The Man
Who Loved
Books
Too Much

VIKING
CANADA

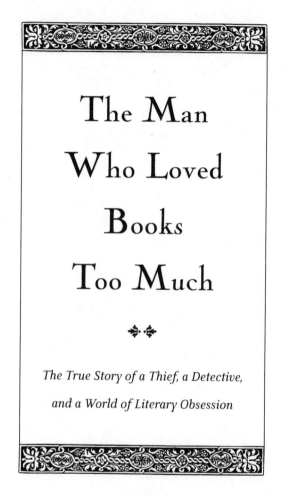

# The Man Who Loved Books Too Much

❖ · ❖

*The True Story of a Thief, a Detective,*
*and a World of Literary Obsession*

ALLISON HOOVER BARTLETT

VIKING CANADA

Published by the Penguin Group

Penguin Group (Canada), 90 Eglinton Avenue East, Suite 700, Toronto,
Ontario, Canada M4P 2Y3 (a division of Pearson Canada Inc.)

Penguin Group (USA) Inc., 375 Hudson Street, New York, New York 10014, U.S.A. •
Penguin Books Ltd, 80 Strand, London WC2R 0RL, England • Penguin Ireland, 25 St
Stephen's Green, Dublin 2, Ireland (a division of Penguin Books Ltd) • Penguin
Group (Australia), 250 Camberwell Road, Camberwell, Victoria 3124, Australia (a
division of Pearson Australia Group Pty Ltd) • Penguin Books India Pvt Ltd, 11
Community Centre, Panchsheel Park, New Delhi–110 017, India • Penguin Group
(NZ), 67 Apollo Drive, Rosedale, North Shore 0632, New Zealand (a division of
Pearson New Zealand Ltd) • Penguin Books (South Africa) (Pty) Ltd,
24 Sturdee Avenue, Rosebank, Johannesburg 2196, South Africa

Penguin Books Ltd, Registered Offices: 80 Strand, London WC2R 0RL, England

Published in Canada by Penguin Group (Canada), a division of Pearson Canada Inc.,
2009. Simultaneously published in the United States by Riverhead Books, a division
of Penguin Group (USA) Inc.

1  3  5  7  9  10  8  6  4  2

*Publisher's note: This book is a work of fiction. Names, characters,
places and incidents either are the product of the author's imagination
or are used fictitiously, and any resemblance to actual persons living or
dead, events, or locales is entirely coincidental.*

Manufactured in the U.S.A.

ISBN: 978-0-670-06799-2

Library and Archives Canada Cataloguing in Publication data available upon request
to the publisher.
American Library of Congress Cataloging in Publication data available.

Visit the Penguin Group (Canada) website at **www.penguin.ca**

Special and corporate bulk purchase rates available; please see **www.penguin.ca/
corporatesales** or call 1-800-810-3104, ext. 477 or 474

BOOK DESIGN BY NICOLE LAROCHE

*For John, Julian, and Sonja*

For him that stealeth, or borroweth and returneth not, this book from its owner . . . let him be struck with palsy, & all his members blasted. . . . Let bookworms gnaw his entrails in token of the Worm that dieth not, & when at last he goeth to his final punishment, let the flames of Hell consume him forever.

*—Anathema in a medieval manuscript*
*from the Monastery of San Pedro in Barcelona*

I have known men to hazard their fortunes, go long journeys halfway about the world, forget friendships, even lie, cheat, and steal, all for the gain of a book.

*—A. S. W. Rosenbach, twentieth-century book dealer*

The Man
Who Loved
Books
Too Much

# *Prologue*

At one end of my desk sits a nearly four-hundred-year-old book cloaked in a tan linen sack and a good deal of mystery. My friend Malcolm came across the book while carrying out the sad task of sorting through his brother's belongings after he committed suicide. On the sack was a handwritten note that began, "To whom it may concern," and went on to explain that several years earlier, a friend had withdrawn the book from a college library where she worked and had accidentally taken it with her when she moved away. He wrote that she had wanted the book to be returned to the library anonymously, but that he hadn't had time to do so. Gingerly, Malcolm lifted the large, heavy tome with gleaming brass clasps from its sack. "Isn't it beautiful?" he said as he handed it to me. My first thought was: Yes, beautiful. My second: It's stolen.

I woke the next morning with the book in my head. Was the story in the note true? If not, where had the book come from? I could see that it was written in German, with a sprinkling of Latin, but what was it about? Was it valuable? Malcolm agreed to let me borrow it for a while. With the help of a German-speaking friend, a librarian, and a rare book dealer, I learned that it was a *Kräutterbuch* ("plant book"[4]) of botanical medicine, by Hieronymus Bock, a botanist and physician. After book burnings in the Middle Ages, knowledge of traditional medicine had been lost, so at the time of the *Kräutterbuch*'s publication, in 1630, the book was a way to return to the old ways of healing, revolutionary for its time.[2]

The *Kräutterbuch* weighs in at twelve pounds, and its cover, oak boards clad in pigskin,[3] is slick but textured with embossed concentric patterns of flowers and leaves and curlicues that have taken on dark shading from the hands of those who have held it. I brought it to San Francisco rare book dealer John Windle, who told me that if you had ordered a copy of a *Kräutterbuch* in the 1600s, you would have paid an extra fee to have the illustrations painted, which the owner of this copy did. The colors, mostly shades of olive or silvery green, mustard yellow, and wine red, were applied sloppily, which Windle informed me is a mark of authenticity; if you come across a meticulously hand-painted copy, there's a good chance it was executed by a bookseller's assistant sometime in the past century in an effort to hike up the book's value.[4] To open the *Kräutterbuch*, you have to squeeze it with two hands, thereby releasing the etched brass clasps shaped like Egyptian columns, flared at the top like regal palm trees. The pages, when turned, make a muffled crack, not unlike the sound of a flag on a windy afternoon, and turning them releases a dry, woody smell, a combination of must and sweetness that I associate with my grandparents' old books. I always link the aroma of an old book to whatever era it was written in, as though its fragrance had emerged directly from the setting of the story. In the case of the *Kräutterbuch*, this scent had traveled a long way in time and space, coming to me from Renaissance Germany. When I run my hand over the pages, I feel subtle waves, presumably warping from moisture, but none of its pages are torn. The blank endpaper is missing, but I learned that this is not unusual. Paper was expensive in the 1600s, and a blank page in a book could be cut out and used as stationery, or for wrapping fish,[5] or for some other more useful purpose than sitting blankly at the front of a book. When I asked Windle about the book's value, he said that because it was in fairly good shape it was worth $3,000 to $5,000. I was pleasantly surprised, although since the book was not mine, I had no rational reason for feeling such satisfaction.

where it was from. I searched the Internet for information about stolen rare books, but while nothing turned up about the *Kräutterbuch*—even the librarian from the library mentioned in the note said that they had no record of it—I stumbled upon something even more intriguing: story after riveting story of theft. Some had occurred weeks or months before, others years ago, in Copenhagen, Kentucky, Cambridge.[7] They involved thieves who were scholars, thieves who were clergymen, thieves who stole for profit, and those whom I found most compelling: smitten thieves who stole purely for the love of books. In several accounts, I came across references to Ken Sanders, a rare book dealer who had become an amateur detective. For three years Sanders had been driven to catch John Gilkey, a man who had become the most successful book thief in recent years. When I contacted Sanders, he said that he had helped put Gilkey behind bars a couple of years earlier, but that he was now free. He had no idea where Gilkey was and doubted that I would have any luck finding him. He also believed that Gilkey was a man who stole out of a love of books. This was the sort of thief whose motivation I might understand. I had to find him.

The more I learned about collectors, the more I began to regard myself as a collector, not of books, but of pieces of this story, and like the people I met who become increasingly rabid and determined as they draw near to completing their book collections, the more information I came across, the more I craved. I learned about vellum and buckram, errata slips and deckled edges. I read about famous inscriptions and forgeries and discoveries. My notebooks grew in number and sat in piles thicker than ten *Kräutterbuch*s stored, as they would have been in 1630, on their sides. As I accumulated information about the thief, the dealer, and the rare book trade, I came to see that this story is not only about a collection of crimes but also about people's intimate and complex and sometimes dangerous relationship to books. For centuries, refined book lovers and greedy con men have brushed up against one another in the rare book world, so in some ways this story is an ancient one. It's also a cautionary tale for those who plan to deal in rare books in the future. It may also be a lesson for those writers who, like me, approach a story with the naive belief that they will be able to follow it the way a spectator passively follows a parade, and that they will be able to leave it without altering its course.

As I wrote this book, the noble *Kräutterbuch* sat in its sack at the end of my desk. I knew my friend wanted to return it, but because the librarian had told me that as far as she knew it was not theirs, I figured, what's the hurry? Besides which, I discovered that if a book has been missing for many years, librarians will sometimes toss the attendant documents—an act of frustration, perhaps, but also of self-protection: they don't want anyone to know they've let a book go missing, especially if it's rare and valuable. The librarian from the *Kräutterbuch*'s supposed home informed me that as they have updated their computer systems, records of the library's holdings have been lost. Maybe this was the case with the *Kräutterbuch*. As weeks, then months, passed and the book was still in my possession, I thought, *I'll deal with it later.* In the meantime, I would open the book and leaf through it. An illustration of an apple tree (*Apffelbaum*) shows, among the fallen fruit at its base, a skull and bone. A poisonous apple! Under another tree, men in caps and knee-length breeches vomit. Next to yet another, cherubic boys wearing nothing but sashes around their copious bellies squat and defecate. On another page, under a different kind of tree, men and women dance drunkenly. Even the illiterate would have had no doubt about each of these plants' effects. Toward the back of the book is one of my favorite illustrations: an elaborate circular depiction of twelve faces representing twelve winds, each from a different direction, and each, cheeks out, blowing its particular remedy or threat. Overlapping this illustration, and throughout the book, are irregular brown blotches, which I learned are called foxing, a book's age spots, usually caused by dampness or

## ❧ 1 ❧

# Like a Moth to a Flame

April 28, 2005, was bright and mild, the kind of spring day in New York City that seems full of promise, and on the corner of Park Avenue and East Sixty-sixth Street a queue of optimistic people was growing. It was opening day of the New York Antiquarian Book Fair, and they were waiting to begin the treasure hunt. The annual fair is held at the Park Avenue Armory, an anachronistic, castle-like building with towers and musket ports that one historian described as large enough to allow a four-abreast formation to march in and out of the building. There were no such formations when I arrived, but a steady stream of book-hungry people marching through the doors, eager to be among the first to see and touch the objects of their desire: modern first editions, illuminated texts, Americana, law books, cookbooks, children's books, World War II histories, incunabula (Latin for "in the cradle," books from printing's infancy, roughly 1450 to 1500[1]), Pulitzer Prize winners, natural histories, erotica, and countless other temptations.

Inside, security guards had taken their positions and were prepared to explain, twice to the indignant, that all but the smallest purses would have to be left behind at the coat check. Overhead lights shone bright and hot, like spotlights aimed at a stage, and as I walked into the fair, I felt like an actor without a script. Ever since I was a teenager, I've been an inveterate flea market shopper, on the prowl for beautiful and interesting objects. Some of my favorite recent finds are an old doctor's bag I use as a purse, wooden forms for ships' gears, which now hang on a wall in my house, and an old watch repairman's kit with glass vials of minuscule parts. (When I was a teen, it was costume jewelry and bootleg eight-track tapes to play in my boyfriend's van.) This book fair was altogether different. A hybrid of museum and marketplace, it was filled with millions of dollars' worth of books and enough weathered leather spines to make a decorator swoon. Collectors strode with purpose toward specific booths, and dealers adjusted the displays of their wares on shelves while eyeing one another's latest and most valuable finds, perched in sparkling glass cases. They even set some of their goods on countertops, where anyone who pleased would be able to pick them up and leaf through them. Everyone but me seemed to know exactly what he was looking for. But what I sought was not as clear-cut as first editions or illuminated manuscripts. I love to read books and I appreciate their aesthetic charms, but I don't collect them; I had come to this fair to understand what makes others do so. I wanted a close-up view into the rare book world, a place where the customs were utterly foreign to me. With any luck—something I'm sure every person at this fair was wishing for—I also hoped to discover something about those whose craving leads them to steal the books they love.

To that end, I was here in part to meet with Ken Sanders, the Salt Lake City rare book dealer and self-styled sleuth I had spoken with on the phone. Sanders has a reputation as a man who relishes catching book thieves, and like a cop who has been on the force for years without a partner, he also savors any opportunity to share a good story. I had called him a few weeks earlier, in preparation for our meeting, and during that first conversation, he had told me about the Red Jaguar Guy, who stole valuable copies of the *Book of Mormon* from him; the Yugoslavian Scammers, whom he helped the FBI track down one weekend; and the Irish Gas Station Gang, who routinely placed fraudulent orders with dealers through the Internet and had them shipped to a gas station in Northern Ireland. But these were preliminary stories, warm-ups for the big one: In 1999, Sanders had begun working as the volunteer security chair of the Antiquarian Booksellers' Association of America. In short, the job was to alert fellow dealers whenever he got wind of a theft so that they could be on the lookout for the missing books. At first, the work was sporadic. Every few months he would receive an e-mail or telephone call about a theft and immediately forward the information to his colleagues. But as time passed, the number of thefts climbed. There seemed to be no one type of book stolen, nor any pattern, except that most had been snatched through credit card fraud. No one knew if this was the work of one thief or a gang of many. Sanders heard from a dealer in the Bay Area who had lost a nineteenth-century diary. The next week, a dealer in Los Angeles reported losing a first-edition *War of the Worlds* by H. G. Wells. Sanders found himself spending less and less time attending to his store and more time trying to figure out what the hell was going on.

Sanders took a deep breath, then launched into a bizarre incident that had occurred at the California International Antiquarian Book Fair in 2003, held in San Francisco. The fair was at the Concourse Exhibition Center, a lackluster, warehouse-like building situated on the edge of the city's design center, just blocks from the county jail—between

showcases for the domestic trappings of wealth and a holding pen for criminals. It was a location that would turn out
to be fitting. With about 250 dealers and 10,000 attendees,
the city's fair is the largest in the world. "That big ol' barn
goes on forever," is how Sanders described it. On opening
day, as usual, collectors and dealers were giddy with a sense
of possibility. Sanders, however, warily paced his booth. He
was surrounded by some of his finest offerings—*The Strategy of Peace*, inscribed by John F. Kennedy, and a first edition
of the *Book of Mormon*—but his mind was not on his books.
Several days before the fair, while sitting in his Salt Lake City
office, surrounded by dusty piles of books and documents,
he had received a phone call from a detective in San Jose,
California. The detective said that the thief Sanders had
spent three years trying to track down (and by then Sanders
had a hunch it was one thief, not a gang) now had a name,
John Gilkey, and that he was in San Francisco.

A couple of days before the fair, Sanders received a mug
shot of Gilkey. He had imagined what the thief looked like,
but this was not it.

"I can tell you one thing," he said. "He didn't look like
Moriarty to me"—referring to the fictional character whom
Sherlock Holmes called the "Napoleon of crime."

The photo showed a plain-looking man in his thirties
with short dark hair parted on the side, a red T-shirt under a

white buttoned shirt, and an expression that was more de-spondent than menacing. Sanders's friend Ken Lopez, a tall Massachusetts dealer with shoulder-length hair and an open pack of Camel cigarettes in his T-shirt pocket, was, as far as they knew, Gilkey's latest victim (he had ordered a first-edition *Grapes of Wrath*). Shortly before the fair opened, Sanders and Lopez talked about handing out Gilkey's photo to all the dealers, even making a wanted poster for the doors of the fair. But Sanders reconsidered. Gilkey's victims, many of whom were at the fair, might one day be called to identify him in a lineup, and Sanders didn't want to risk contami-nating the process. All he could do was remain vigilant and wonder if Gilkey would be brazen enough to show up at the fair.

"I was thinking that he would be attracted to a good fair like a moth to a flame," he said. "And he would be there to steal books."

The San Francisco fair had been open less than an hour when Sanders locked eyes with a man he didn't recognize. This was not so unusual. Sanders often forgets names, even faces. But this encounter was different.

"I looked at that guy, and he looked right back into my eyes," said Sanders, "and I got the weirdest goddamn feeling."

It was not the mug shot he was thinking of. That had already faded from his memory. Something else had snagged his attention, a strange, sure sense that flooded him in a slice of a second. Sanders's daughter, Melissa, was helping a customer at the other end of the booth, and Sanders turned to ask her to take a look at this dark-haired, ordinary-looking man he suspected was Gilkey. But when Sanders turned around to point out the man to Melissa, he had vanished.

Sanders rushed down the aisle, past four or five other booths, bumping into a couple of collectors along the way, to his friend John Crichton's booth. Still stunned, he paused to catch his breath. "I think I just saw Gilkey," Sanders told him.

"You've got to relax, old man," Crichton said, reaching out to pat him on the shoulder. "You're getting paranoid."

❖ ❖

SO IT WAS with all of this in mind that I wandered through the New York fair, waiting for my scheduled meeting with Sanders at his booth, and wondering, as I observed the scene around me, if any of these people were like Gilkey. What about the elderly man at a counter a few feet away looking back and forth from one blood-red leather-bound book to another almost identical one? Or the dark-suited couple whispering to each other as they ogled a book on nineteenth-century French architecture? It was hard not to view everyone with suspicion, but I tried to keep my imagination in check as I approached my first booth.

Straight ahead was Aleph-Bet Books, where I was drawn in by an enticing array of children's books, first editions of many that I recognized from my childhood, like *Pinocchio*, although this was a first edition in Italian, which at $80,000 cost around twenty thousand times more than my own childhood copy at home (a Golden Book). The booth was packed with hungry collectors, but I managed to get the attention of co-owner Marc Younger, who explained to me why so many fairgoers had crowded his booth. People have an emotional attachment to books they remember reading as children, he said, and very often it's the first type of book a collector seeks. Some move on to other books, but many spend a lifetime collecting their favorite childhood stories. He showed me the first trade edition of *The Tale of Peter Rabbit* ($15,000).

"It's an interesting story," he said. "No one would publish it, so she [Beatrix Potter] self-published two hundred and fifty of them. They go up to a hundred thousand dollars."

Next, he pointed out a first-edition *The Cat in the Hat*, priced at $8,500. It looked pretty much like a new *The Cat in the Hat* to me, and he confirmed that it can be difficult to identify first editions of children's books, in part because the edition is not always noted. Apparently, you have to look for other clues. Younger explained that when first published, *The Cat in the Hat's* boards (a term for covers—I was learning the lingo) were covered in flat paper, but that later they were glazed (shiny). I was starting to feel like an insider. At the next flea market, I could be on the lookout for a first-edition *The Cat in the Hat.*

Younger then agreed to show me something more rare. He had two letters from L. Frank Baum, author of the Wizard of Oz books, to John R. Neill, who illustrated many of them. "Usually it's the really extraordinary things that do well," he said, "like these." Younger expected them to go for $45,000 to $60,000. So many of his books (not to mention the letters, original illustrations, and other ephemera) seemed like "really extraordinary things" that I walked away with a kind of book-fever setting in.

Across the aisle from Aleph-Bet were the largest books I'd ever seen: sumptuously illustrated volumes of natural history, as big as coffee tables and twice as thick, which the dealer, a bow-tied gentleman who spoke in hushed tones, called elephant folios. Based on size and weight, they were aptly named, and I wondered where, other than museums, such books would be useful, or even practical to lug from a shelf, for example, to a table. After admiring a darkly lush, eerie floral illustration in one of the elephant folios, "The Night-Blowing Cereus," by Robert John Thornton (1799), I left and headed in the other direction, to a booth where I got to see a rare first edition of Beethoven's Fifth Symphony ($13,500) and a valuable copy of *Molecular Structure of Nucleic Acids*, Watson and Crick's first and second DNA article offprints, signed ($140,000).

The New York fair guidebook indicated that Sanders was in booth D8. Making my way there, I stopped by several more booths. At Bruce McKittrick Rare Books of Philadelphia, owner McKittrick was charming anyone who stopped by with his rapid-fire musings on books. His booth attracted more people than any around it, but that may also have been due to the champagne he poured. He told me about Pietro Aretino, a sixteenth-century Italian writer whose oeuvre included erotic books. In 1524, he wrote a collection of sonnets to accompany the engravings of sixteen sexual positions by Marcantonio Raimondi (who based his images on a series of paintings by Giulio Romano, a student of Raphael's). It remains one of the most famous examples of Renaissance erotica.

"The original editions of his books are so rare and were read to death and were extremely scandalous," said McKittrick, "not just slightly pornographic. Not like eighteenth-century French soft porn. In Venice, in the 1520s, so many wanted it, the stuff just disappeared."

He said people pirated Aretino's work, and at the fair he was selling a mid-seventeenth-century fake of a pirated copy.

"A fake of a fake," he said. "Very interesting."

Before the fair, I had learned that there are probably as many definitions of "rare" as there are book dealers. Most tend toward the cheeky. Burt Auerback, a Manhattan appraiser, is quoted as having said, "It is a book that is worth more money now than when it was published."[2] The late American collector Robert H. Taylor said that a rare book is "a book I want badly and can't find."[3] On the occasions that people answer seriously, they all agree that "rare" is a highly subjective moniker.

The earliest use of the term has been traced to an English book-sale catalog in November 1692.[4] But it wasn't until the early eighteenth century that scholars attempted to define what makes a book rare, with bibliophile J. E. Berger making Monty Python–esque distinctions between *"rarus"* and *"rarior"* and *"rarissiumus."*[5] A book's degree of rarity remains subjective, and the only qualities of "rare" that collectors and dealers seem to agree on is some combination of scarcity, importance, and condition. Taste and trends play roles as well, however. When a movie adaptation is released, whether *Pride and Prejudice* or *Nancy Drew*, first editions of the book often become temporarily hot property among collectors. While Dickens will almost certainly be a perennial choice, Dr. Seuss's star has risen as the children who were raised on his books have become adults with the means to form their own collections.[6]

———————

Walking by a booth with an impressive selection of dust jacket art, I heard a dealer say to a passerby, "Don't judge a book by its content!" I had read enough about book collectors before the fair to get the joke: Many collectors don't actually read their books. At first, I was surprised, but having given it some thought, it's not so shocking. After all, much of the fondness avid readers, and certainly collectors, have for their books is related to the books' physical bodies. As much as they are vessels for stories (and poetry, reference information, etc.), books are historical artifacts and repositories for memories—we like to recall who gave books to us, where we were when we read them, how old we were, and so on.

For me, the most important book-as-object from my childhood is *Charlotte's Web*, the first book I mail-ordered after joining a book club. I still remember my thrill at seeing the mailman show up with it at our front door on a sunny Saturday morning. It had a crisp paper jacket, unlike the plastic-covered library books I was used to, and the way the pages parted, I could tell I was the first to open it. For several days I lived in Wilbur's world, and the only thing as sad as Charlotte's death, maybe even sadder, was that I had come to the end of the book. I valued that half-dream state of being lost in a book so much that I limited the number of pages I let myself read each day in order to put off the inevitable end, my banishment from that world. I still do this. It doesn't make sense, though, because the pleasure of that world does not really end for good. You can always start over on page one—and you can remember. Whenever I have spotted my old *Charlotte's Web* (on my son's shelf, then my daughter's), I have recalled how it came to me. It's a personal record of one chapter of my life, just as other chapters have other books I associate with them. The pattern continues; my daughter returned from camp last summer with her copy of *Motherless Brooklyn* in a state approaching ruin. She told me she'd dropped it into a creek, but couldn't bear to leave it behind, even after she'd finished it. This book's body is inextricably linked to her experience of reading it. I hope that she continues to hold on to it, because as long as she does, its wavy, expanded pages will remind her of the hot day she read it with her feet in the water—and of the fourteen-year-old she was at the time. A book is much more than a delivery vehicle for its contents, and from my perspective, this fair was a concentrated celebration of that fact.

❖·❖

AT THE REFRESHMENT STAND toward the back of the fair, I overheard one man say he had just seen Al Pacino, and someone else note that he had spotted one of the *Antiques Roadshow* experts. The appeal of that PBS show (your junk may be really, really valuable!) was also one of the appeals of the fair. Nothing looked like junk, but plenty of the modern first editions looked perfectly ordinary. Several times I wondered, *Do I still have that book? Do my parents? Could it be a first edition?*

As I continued to make my way through the fair, the dealers I talked to seemed more excited about the *Roadshow* man than about Pacino. Still, I took note of every dark-haired man walking by, hoping for a movie star. Pacino certainly would have blended into the crowd better than I, a woman. Most of the collectors were men,[7] most well over forty. Many appeared to be scholars or aged hippies or lucky book lovers with inheritances burning holes in their pockets. One man's red Porsche is one of these guys' inscribed first-edition copies of *Portnoy's Complaint.* When handling any of these books, they cradled them, half open, in both hands, so as not to split the spines or cause any other trauma—no rips or folds or coffee spills. They consulted guides and maps of the fair floor, squinted through spectacles across booths, and stooped to better run their eyes down the spines of books, trying to locate a copy of a first edition of *Harry Potter and the Philosopher's Stone*, of which there were only five hundred printed ($30,000), for example, or the very rare first edition of *The History of the Expedition Under the Command of Captains Lewis and Clark* ($139,000). Those with less extravagant means were probably hunting down more modest prizes, like a first edition of Toni Morrison's *Beloved* ($125) or, more affordable yet, a first edition of John Updike's *Rabbit Is Rich* ($45).[8] They also must have been roaming the aisles hoping to be surprised, because that's any treasure hunter's dream—in this case, to stumble upon a book whose scarcity or beauty or history or provenance is even more seductive than the story printed between its covers.

At a fair like this, it's obvious that the allure of any book is in large part sensual. I watched collectors feast their eyes, their hands, their noses. An Englishman placed his coffee cup at a safe distance on the counter before taking a good whiff of a copy of *Alice's Adventures in Wonderland*, then fell into the rabbit hole of John Tenniel's enchanting illustrations. Watching him, I assumed he simply liked the smell of old books, but later I learned that sniffing is also a practical precaution: mildew can ravage a book, and a good whiff can tell you if there's any danger of its encroachment.[9] As I roamed from booth to booth, book to book, I felt the sensory enticement myself—the feel of thick, rough-edged pages, the sharp beauty of type, the tightness of linen or pigskin covers, the papery smell.

In my pre-fair research, I learned that this fondness not only for rare books but also for endlessly acquiring them has been alive for twenty-five centuries.[10] Around 400 B.C., Euripides was mocked for his appetite for books.[11] A few hundred years later, Cicero noted that he was "saving up all my little income" to develop his collection.[12] In the "golden age of collecting," roughly 1870 to 1930, the world was teeming with fevered collectors. They were and are a determined breed, and their desire can swell from an innocent love of books, or bibliophilia, to an affliction far more rabid, bibliomania, a term coined by the Reverend Frognall Dibdin in 1809.[13] An English bibliographer and avid collector, Dibdin noted that "what renders it particularly formidable is that it rages in all seasons of the year, and at all periods of human existence."[14] When the books, like those at the New York fair, have pasts—secret, scandalous, or sweet—the attraction is that much more robust. That they also hold history, poetry, science, and stories on their pages can seem almost secondary. The fair was abuzz with people fully in the grip of the spell they cast.

This spell is made even more potent by stories of discovery that collectors share. One of my favorites happened on a spring day in 1988.[15] That morning, a Massachusetts man who collected books about local history was rummaging through a bin in a New Hampshire antiques barn when something caught his eye. Beneath texts on fertilizers and farm machines lay a slim, worn pamphlet with tea-colored paper covers, titled *Tamerlane and Other Poems*, by an unnamed author identified simply as "a Bostonian." He was

fairly certain he had found something exceptional, paid the
$15 price, and headed home, where *Tamerlane* would spend
only one night. The next day, he contacted Sotheby's, and
they confirmed his suspicion that he had just made one of
the most exciting book discoveries in years. The pamphlet
was a copy of Edgar Allan Poe's first text, written when he
was only fourteen years old, a find that fortune-seeking collectors have imagined happening upon probably more often
than they'd like to admit. The humble-looking, forty-page
pamphlet was published in 1827 by Calvin F. S. Thomas, a
relatively unknown Boston printer who specialized in apoth-
ecary labels, and its original price was about twelve cents.
But this copy, looking good for its 161 years, most of which
were probably spent languishing in one dusty attic box after
another, would soon be auctioned for a staggering $198,000.
The value of *Tamerlane*, which caused no stir when it was
first published and was never even reviewed, has nothing to
do with its literary merit, but rather its association with a
seminal author, and every time a copy has been unearthed,
the price has skyrocketed. Estimates of how many copies of
*Tamerlane* were printed range from fifty to five hundred, but
so far only fourteen known copies have surfaced, most of
which are held in public institutions. In the 1890s, a dealer
in Boston spied it on another dealer's ten-cent table, and
later sold it for $1,000. In the 1950s, the unassuming text

articulate dealer from Switzerland. Even in a crowd of erudite, bookish people, he stood out. In the first few minutes of our conversation, he mentioned Nietzsche, Goethe, and Florentine architects. From a glass case, he retrieved a manuscript, unbound, in a shallow box. He had acquired it at auction in 2004, where it had been described simply as "a full work of Flaubert, 254 pages." It had been priced "idiotically low," said Moirandat. "I was desperate. Like many in this business, I'm undercapitalized, but it was so ridiculously cheap. I think people must have misread the description, maybe thought it was only twenty-five pages. I decided to put in a bid. . . . I got it at half the price."

He opened the box and, to my surprise, invited me to leaf through the slightly yellowed pages. They were written in brown ink, which had faded somewhat, as had the drips and splatters, and many lines had been aggressively crossed out. Moirandat said it was a piece Flaubert supposedly wrote while traveling, although he doubted it.

"I'm convinced he didn't write it on the trip. It's too well formed."

He read a passage aloud in French, then translated it roughly for me.

"I will abstain from every declamation and I will not allow myself more than six times per page to use the word 'picturesque' and only a dozen times the word 'admirable.'

I want my sentences to smell of the leather of my travel-ing shoes . . ."

"It is like peeking in the workshop," sighed Moirandat, looking over my shoulder at the manuscript.

I had to agree. Its unfinished state, with words scratched out and ink spilled, gave it an immediate, intimate quality. Moirandat left me with the manuscript for a few minutes while he helped a customer. I touched the pages and realized how much I would love to own something like it. *This is how it happens,* I thought. I could slip these sheets under my sweater and make a dash for the door. As I waited for Moiran-dat to return, I noticed other handsome items he had left on the counter. He was not acting carelessly. Almost every dealer I'd visited so far had done this. When Moirandat returned, I had to stop myself from suggesting he not be so trusting. I might as well suggest to a Japanese host that guests keep their shoes on. Trust was clearly part of the rare book trade's culture, and who was I to suggest resisting it?

When I asked Moirandat if he had ever suffered a theft, he told me how he once traveled to Germany in pursuit of a thief who had taken a volume from his store in Basel. When Moirandat caught up with him, the thief denied he had been in Basel at the time of the theft. But Moirandat knew his books' physical markings as intimately as a parent knows a child's freckles and scars. In court, he told the judge, who held the book in question, to turn to page 28. "You will find three small holes there, and if you go to the last page, you will find my predecessor's entry mark." The judge did, and the suspect, a public school teacher, was convicted.

Moirandat also told me about a man who had used the "wet string" method.

"He went one day to the library with a length of wool yarn hidden in his cheek. He placed the wet yarn inside a book, along the spine," he said. "He put the book back on the shelf and came back a few weeks later. As the yarn dried, it grew shorter, which made a clean cut."

The thief didn't have to smuggle a razor in. A length of wet yarn was all he needed to walk away with one valuable page: an original Manet print. Later, he went to Moirandat's shop and tried to sell him a book. "It was the absolute rarest Goethe first edition that there is on the cathedral in Salzburg. It's one of the really, really great texts by Goethe, seminal to the development of romanticism. It had a round library stamp, eighteen millimeters in diameter, which he had tried to erase. I could see the stamp, but couldn't tell which library it was from. I called up every Swiss library until I found where it was from." The police were notified, and the man, thief of Manet and Goethe, was caught.

I walked away thinking it's a wonder this sort of thing doesn't happen all the time.

I passed McKittrick's booth again, and he motioned for me to wait a moment while he quickly crossed the aisle to speak with dealer Sebastiaan Hesselink of the Netherlands. When McKittrick had told me earlier about the pirated fake Aretino, I had asked him about other crimes in the trade, like theft. He hadn't had any stories for me, which is why he was now talking to Hesselink. McKittrick asked him if he would speak to me about, he whispered, *the theft.* He would, so McKittrick introduced us. I guessed that not all dealers might be willing to share a story of theft, so I felt fortunate that Hesselink had agreed to it. While his son manned their booth, Hesselink and I left the fair floor and sat on folding chairs in a dark, quiet hallway off the foyer.

In a distinctive Dutch accent, Hesselink described how several years earlier, a man had called him and asked if he would be interested in some very rare items, including a Book of Hours and letters from several American presidents. Hesselink was interested, but as soon as he saw the books, he became suspicious. He lives in the countryside outside Amsterdam, "in the middle of nowhere," yet here was a man from New York who had traveled that great distance to sell him books that could have been sold easily in the United States.

"This was already fishy," said Hesselink, who said he became more cautious than usual.

He looked at all the materials and made an offer, which the man immediately accepted. This, too, was strange, he said. In order to stall, Hesselink told the man that because the banks had already closed, he could write a check, knowing that the man would prefer cash, and then suggested they meet the next day, when Hesselink would be able to offer it. Immediately after the man left, Hesselink contacted colleagues in the United States to see if they knew of any stolen books that resembled what he had just been offered. It took only hours to discover that all of the materials had been stolen from Columbia University. Hesselink contacted Interpol, the FBI, and local Dutch authorities, and they set up a sting for four o'clock the next day in the town's public square.

The story seemed straight out of a mystery novel, and my favorite detail was yet to come: That night, Hesselink and his son cut stacks of newspaper into rectangles the size of gilder notes and put bundles of them—the "payment"—into a plastic garbage bag. At four the next day, the man arrived in Utrecht's central square with his bag of loot. Police, in bulletproof vests, had surrounded the area. Hesselink suggested that the man accompany him to Hesselink's car, where the payment was. After a number of Keystone Kops–style blunders by local police, they managed to arrest him. Prosecuting him would turn out to be even more problematic.[17]

I asked Hesselink if he was frightened while handing over the bag of "money," since the man could have been armed and the police might not have acted fast enough, but he said

able, beloved books that collectors have hired them to sell, they don't want to risk being seen as vulnerable.

I had brought a slim notebook to the fair and already wished I'd brought a thicker one. Every dealer had a different story to tell. The only thing I heard more than once was, "Every rare book is a stolen book." The Nazis were rampant pillagers of collections, dealers explained, as were the Romans, who stole whole libraries from the Greeks, and Queen Christina of Sweden, who collected a vast booty during the Thirty Years' War.[18] But they were referring also to thieves who act on their own behalf. Whether by the hands of conquerors or corrupt collectors, valuable books go missing, and unless a thief tries to sell a book to a reputable dealer or institution shortly after swiping it, they told me, there's a good chance that no one will be able to track it down. Eventually, perhaps a year later, a decade later, a century later, the book is sold to someone who has no knowledge of its past, no idea of its tainted provenance. It is impossible to track the history of ownership of every book. This, I assumed, is something any clever book thief has figured out.

I turned a corner and spotted Ken Sanders's booth. I was eager to see the face of the impressive storyteller. He did not blend in with the rare book fair crowd any better than I. Sanders has an ample paunch, a thinning ponytail, and a long black-and-white beard that he strokes and twists between his thumb and fingers. His eyebrows form sharp inverted V's over his eyes, making him look curious or indignant; I would soon learn that he very often is one or the other. While he has a suffer-no-fools way about him, if you're interested in a book or a story, he has all the time in the world. He calls himself the "Book Cop." His friends call him "Bibliodick."

We sat in two chairs at the edge of his booth and talked about how things were going at the fair.

"In a fair like this," he said, "I'm a bottom-feeder. Not like those up on Park Avenue."

That's what Sanders called the aisles up near the front of the fair, which is prohibitively expensive for all but the high-end rare book dealers. Sanders, who told me he attends six to eight fairs a year, is an egalitarian and prefers the San Francisco fair, where a dealer's booth location is decided by lottery. "A lot of New Yorkers hate it," he said. "They'd rather have it be all elite. I like the mixture." I mentioned the rumor that Al Pacino was shopping for books, but he was uninterested. He said that twice, at previous fairs, he had spoken to longtime collector Steve Martin (once, while almost backing into Diane Keaton), but hadn't realized who Martin (or Keaton) was until his daughter, Melissa, exasperatedly informed him, twice.

I asked how things were going.

"We started unpacking at nine A.M. yesterday," said Sanders. "Other dealers will help you unpack to see what you've got. So much depends on your knowledge, though."

He told me about a book he saw one dealer sell to another for $200 that morning, then watched the dealer resell it for $3,500 that afternoon. One dealer had recognized value where the other had not.

We hadn't been sitting for more than a couple of minutes when Sanders told me about the first New York fair he exhibited at.

"Ten minutes into opening night, I lost a thousand-dollar book. And my friend Rob Rulon-Miller lost a book by Roger Williams worth thirty-five thousand. The two of us marched over to the Nineteenth Precinct, which is literally out the back door of the Armory. You can imagine a New York police precinct. And the two of us in *suits* over there. I let Rob go first."

Sanders explained that dealers are used to police scoffing at news of a stolen book, especially when it's worth a lot of money. "People pay that for a *book*?" they ask skeptically.

"Me, being the smart one," continued Sanders, "I let Rob break the ice and explain to the sergeant on duty that we were there to report book thefts. When Rob gives him the details, the sergeant looks up at him, disbelievingly, and says, 'Roger *Williams*? You talking about one of the guys who founded Rhode Island?' He actually knew who the man was. I was very impressed. Then he says, 'You let someone walk away with a first-edition *Roger Williams*?!' And he looked at Rob like: You're some kinda moron, right? After that, I decided my thousand-dollar book wasn't worth making a fuss about."

Moving on to more recent crimes, Sanders said that based on all the theft notices he had received from fellow dealers, he estimates that from the end of 1999 to the beginning of 2003, John Gilkey stole about $100,000 worth of books from dealers around the country. In the past decade, no other thief has been anywhere near that prolific. What was even more unusual, though, was that none of the items Gilkey stole later showed up for sale on the Internet or at any other public venue. It was this, combined with the inconsistency of Gilkey's targeted titles (spanning a wide variety of genres and time periods) and the fact that some of the books he stole were not very valuable, that had Sanders convinced that he actually stole for love. Gilkey loved the books and wanted to own them. But Sanders couldn't prove it.

Weeks earlier, when we had first spoken on the phone, Sanders had told me he was fairly certain that Gilkey had already served time at San Quentin State Prison and that he was now free. He shuddered at the thought, warning me that it would be difficult if not impossible to find Gilkey.

The day after that phone conversation, I looked into it.[19] As Sanders had presumed, Gilkey had indeed done time at San Quentin and had been released. What Sanders did not know was that he was again behind bars, this time in a prison in Tracy, California. I wrote Gilkey a letter asking if he would talk to me. Knowing that he had denied his thefts in court, I didn't expect him to open up to me about them. In the letter, I told him that I was interested in writing a story about people who have gone to extraordinary lengths to get rare books. It was a euphemism I hoped would keep him from feeling defensive.

While waiting for a reply, I ordered several books about book collecting and read a stack of articles. One of them, from *The Age*, an Australian newspaper, stuck with me because it indicated that book thievery was rampant.[20] Why hadn't I heard about this? Why hadn't any of the friends I asked? The 2003 story was about how those in charge of the Secret Archives of the Vatican, an underground vault holding eighty-five kilometers of historical papers, illuminated manuscripts, antediluvian books, and rare correspondence, have to be on guard against thieves. This was intriguing enough, but there was one sentence in particular that caught my eye: an Interpol agent, Vivianna Padilla, revealed that according to the global police agency's statistics, book theft is more widespread than fine art theft.

Something else caught my attention. It was an online reference to the Antiquarian Booksellers' Association of America's profiles of five types of book thieves: the kleptomaniac who cannot keep himself from stealing; the thief who steals for profit; the thief who steals in anger; the casual thief; and the thief who steals for his own personal use. The ABAA had defined them, I suppose, to help dealers and librarians recognize and protect against the range of motivations that might drive a thief. *Know thine enemy.* Of all these, the one that interested me most was the thief who steals for his own personal use—one who steals out of a desire for books. How different would such a person be from the typical book collector? They all seem to be passionate and driven by want. A few dealers had already confided to me that in decades of working with rare books, they had been tempted more than once to steal a book, but had found the strength to resist it. At the book fair, I saw how easy it could be to walk away with something truly unique and wondrous (Flaubert's own papers!). What makes someone cross the line from admirer to thief, and how fine is that line? I wanted to find out.

After several weeks of checking my mailbox, I found what I had been hoping for—an envelope stamped diagonally in large red letters: STATE PRISON GENERATED MAIL. Inside was a letter written in fine, small print on lined paper.

*Yes,* wrote Gilkey, *I would be delighted to tell my story.*

With the letter, he sent a page ripped from a Department of Corrections regulations handbook. He had drawn two stars next to the section titled "Media Access to Facilities" and written in the margin, *It's easy to get approved!*

❖❖

SITTING OUTSIDE SANDERS'S BOOTH at the New York fair, I watched him talk to customers, some of whom he knew well, others not at all. In either case, he was an accommodating host, taking pleasure in sharing his books with people who appreciated them. Again, I had the impression that the book fair was a kind of theater, and Sanders, a seasoned player. When his booth emptied for a minute, he sat down next to me again.

"Gilkey wrote to me from prison," I decided to tell him, "and said he's willing to speak with me."

For a moment, Sanders didn't respond. I had expected him to be excited about the news, eager to hear the details (this, after all, was his big quarry), but instead he looked stern, incredulous. Before saying anything, he gave me a sideways glance.

"You should ask him where all the books he stole are hidden," he said, peevishly. "I bet he's got a storage unit somewhere out in Modesto, where he's from." He stared at the floor a moment, then added, "He's not going to tell you, of course."

It had been over two years since Gilkey had stolen books from Sanders's colleagues, but Sanders was obviously still stung by the experience. Unlike me, merely intrigued by the idea of Gilkey's thefts, Sanders's way of life had been violated by them. He had a legitimate grievance against Gilkey. It was time for me to go, but before I left his booth, Sanders needed to give me one more warning:

"I tell you," he said, knowing I would soon meet with Gilkey, "all, and I mean all, book thieves are natural-born liars."

# ❧ 2 ❧

# Half-truths

When I returned to San Francisco, I found in my mailbox another envelope stamped STATE PRISON GENERATED MAIL. Inside, Gilkey had written more encouragement and information regarding visiting hours (weekends only), that his time in prison was soon to end (in July), and that *it might be a good idea for you to call DVI [the prison] and set a date.* I did.

Deuel Vocational Institution lies sixty-five miles east of San Francisco, in Tracy. On the late spring day I drove there, the sky was a dull blue, the wind fierce, and the hills well on their way to a dry shade of brown. Off the highway, the frontage road was bordered by Harley-Davidsons, powerboats, and off-road vehicles in various states of disrepair. I turned onto Casson Road, which led to the prison, a group of beige two- and three-story buildings surrounded by two layers of razor-wire fencing.

It was nine-fifteen in the morning and already hot. I told a uniformed woman behind the window at the Reception Center that I was there for my appointment. "We'll call you when it's your turn," she grunted, adding that if I had any change, it would have to be in a plastic bag, and that I couldn't bring any paper money inside. So before joining the people waiting in the lobby, I ran out to my car and locked my cash in the glove compartment.

I had never been inside a prison, but I'd heard stories from a friend who had conducted an interview in one. The women visiting, she explained, were dressed to the nines, usually in very low-cut, tight blouses, and the atmosphere thrummed with lust and danger.

Inside the DVI Reception Center, the atmosphere was more church social than sleazy bar. Parents, spouses, grandparents, and children, mostly Hispanic, sat and waited to hear their names called. Occasionally, one of them would drift over to the corner, where there was a gift shop with in-mates' crafts for sale. A painting of a terrified-looking wolf with yellow eyes hung on a wall above three identical wooden wishing well lamps for $24 each and a selection of clocks with pictures of Jesus or desert scenes lacquered to their faces.

I had been waiting over an hour, trying to distract myself from the growing knot in my stomach. What if Gilkey was more hostile than I expected? Would I be safe talking to him? I stared at the wall, to which several handwritten signs were taped: "No Levi's" and "No sleeveless tops" and "No sandals." Another one read "No underwire bras." They must set off the metal detectors. I ran back across the hot parking lot into my car, sank low in my seat, wrestled off my bra, and pulled it out one sleeve. I was glad I had not worn a white blouse. I ran back in. A half-hour later my name was called.

When I finally got through the metal detector and two sets of heavily locked doors, I arrived in the visiting room and walked to the desk to announce who I was there to see. I waited for what seemed like hours while officials located Gilkey, wanting more than anything to have the interview over with. At last, they found him and brought him to the booth, where he sat behind a Plexiglas window. I approached, trying to look as though I did this all the time. He was dressed in a prison-issued V-necked orange shirt with a threadbare undershirt showing at the neck, and orange elastic-waist pants. He smiled and tipped his head as if to say, "Please, take a seat." I told myself this was a good sign; he didn't appear to be angry—yet. I was still in my coat and sweating from heat and nerves. I glanced at the list of questions in my notebook, which began with nonconfrontational topics: Where did you grow up? When did you first become interested in rare books? And so on. At the end of the list, I had written: *Did you steal any books?* But I figured I would probably have to wait until another day to ask that one. I introduced myself through the heavy black phone receiver on my side of the glass, and he, apparently as nervous as I, quickly said hello. Then, just as abruptly, he offered, "So, do you want me to tell you how I got my first book?"

I exhaled and began writing. At the time of our first meeting Gilkey was thirty-seven. He is of average stature, about five-foot-nine. His eyes are hazel-brown, his hair dark and thinning, his fingers long and nail-bitten. The cadence of his quiet, calm voice reminded me of the children's television host Mr. Rogers. Trying not to think about the resemblance, I asked him how he first became interested in books.

"My family has this big library in the family room with thousands of books, and I remember looking at them all the time," he said. "Also, I used to watch those British Victorian movies, you know, like Sherlock Holmes. I loved those movies where a gentleman has an old library, wears a smoking jacket."

Exploring his motives seemed to please Gilkey, but there was nothing revelatory about it: he seemed comfortable in this knowledge of himself, that his fantasy of living an old-fashioned, cultured English life as depicted on the big screen is what compelled him to steal books.

"Watching those movies," he said, "that was when I first thought about getting books."

Gilkey smiled and shrugged as if he knew that his pronouncement sounded a bit ridiculous, but it was the truth. If you aren't born into learned, wealthy society, why not steal your way in? His affable manner was disturbingly at odds with the content of our discussion, but it made questioning him easier than I had expected.

Since prison rules prohibited my bringing a pen or tape recorder (more metal), I wrote at hand-cramping speed with a pencil I feared would snap since I had sharpened it to a long point (no spares allowed). I tried to tune out the two women on either side of me who, in vehemently cheerful voices, shared whatever good news of home they could scrounge up, while Gilkey told me about his favorite bookstore.

"In the late 1990s, the primary bookstore I went to was a great store in L.A., Heritage Books. It's housed in a converted mausoleum. You have to see it," he said. Later, I would learn that he not only "went to" Heritage, but stole from it.

The Heritage Book Shop, which closed in 2007, was, I found out, one of the most successful rare book businesses in the country, founded by brothers Ben and Lou Weinstein, two former junk-store owners who found their way into the rare book trade in the 1960s.[1] With stained-glass windows,

English cabinets, and a vaulted ceiling, the store exuded old-world wealth. New-world, Hollywood-style wealth was evident in the chairs, which had been used as set furniture in the film *Gone With the Wind*. This combination of old-time finery and movie-business glamour was irresistible to Gilkey, who thought that if he ever opened a bookstore, one of his dreams, he would like it to look like Heritage.

"I guess I got a warped sense of what was possible in that place," he said. "I started dreaming of building a gigantic library, where I will sit at a nice desk. I'll read or write. I'll have a globe of the world next to the desk," he added, unaware of how revealing his change in tense was.

"At Heritage," he said, "that's where I got the idea of owning a collection."

He had already said that he was first inspired to build a collection as a child, but I didn't interrupt. Gilkey was eager to tell his story, so from then on, I asked few questions. He was soft-spoken, pleasant, almost courtly, and forthcoming about how he built his book collection, yet averse to using words like "steal" or "prison" or "theft." Instead, he "got" books and has been "away" for "doing that." He seemed intelligent, but frequently mispronounced words the way well-read people who have not grown up around well-read people often do.

Gilkey said he collects more than rare books: snuff bottles, musical instruments, baseball cards, crystal, coins, and autographs, noting that he has Stephen King's, Anne Perry's, Princess Diana's, and Ronald Reagan's. But it was clear that his attraction was primarily to books, and I would learn that in this respect, Gilkey is typical of collectors, who very often accumulate more than one type of object. They have a focus, though, and Gilkey's unequivocally was books. But why? And what made his desire so fervid that he was willing to risk his freedom for it? Gilkey returned to the image of an English gentleman with a grand library and explained further.

"I like the feeling of having a book worth five or ten grand in my hands. And there's that sense of admiration you're gonna get from other people."

That people would admire Gilkey because of his book collection seemed to be at the crux of his desire. It wasn't merely a love of books that compelled him, but also what owning them would say about him. It's a normal ambition—that our choice of music or cars or shoes reflects well on us—taken to the extreme. Having spent a few days among collectors and dealers at the New York Antiquarian Book Fair, I sensed that many of them were also building identities through their collections, acquiring books as talismans of taste, knowledge, and affluence. Shortly before visiting Gilkey, while flipping through a magazine, I noticed an advertisement for a wealth management company in which a well-dressed woman was leaving a rare book store. Around the same time, I received a hip women's clothing catalog in which at least half the photographs were shot in an old library. In both cases, fine, old books were the backdrop of the good life, the wealthy life, one rich with country estates and long vacations in foreign countries. It's a seductive fantasy that if you acquire the books, you might just end up with the life itself, or at least make other people think you have it. In my research, I had read about other motivations. Some collectors (of cereal boxes, farm machinery, anything) describe their obsession as a way to create order and to fill a hole in their lives.[2] But don't most people crave at least some order? And don't many have a hole of some sort in their lives—unhappy childhoods or health problems or marital woes? Again, this impulse seems like a normal one taken to the extreme. In many ways, Gilkey did not appear to be all that different from other book collectors. The only quality I knew of that set him apart was his criminal history.

The more Gilkey spoke, the more incongruities emerged. The combination of his full, round face and thinning dark hair made him appear at once young and old. He was unevenly shaven but careful in his manner, which made him seem both lost and deliberate. And most striking, he collected books to feel "grand, regal, like royalty, rich, cultured," yet has become a criminal, stealing in order to give himself the appearance of wealth and erudition.

We had only thirty minutes, and Gilkey happily plowed

through his story, jumping back and forth in time, guided by memories of various books he stole rather than by chronology. It appeared that he wanted to cover a lot of ground. Maybe, like me, he thought it might be our only conversation. When the subject turned to his release from prison and what he might do, he laid out his plans.

"I'm full of creativity," he said. "When you're in here twenty-four/seven, you get a lot of ideas." He noted them in quick succession:

"I want one book from each famous author.

"I want to write the presidential library and see if they'll send me a book.

"I'm going to put an ad in the paper. It will say 'Keep me out of jail: send me a book.'

"I'm gonna open a bookstore.

"I've actually written a long book. It was inspired by the work of John Kendrick Bangs. He wrote nineteenth-century prose and plays. I drafted an homage to him. And a couple of suspense stories."

Gilkey was in prison this time because only three weeks after being released, following a three-year sentence for book theft, he went to a book fair and wrote a bad check. He does not like being in prison. "I stand out like a sore thumb," he said, and intimated that he has fended off sexual assaults. Watching Gilkey through the Plexiglas window, as though I felt the awkward boy at the front of the class with the too-short pants and neatly combed hair had somehow found himself amid rapists and carjackers.

"The intellectual level is low here," he said. "I went to college, UC Santa Cruz.[3] I've had an extremely rough time here." Still, he found time to read. "I'm reading Tom Clancy. My first cellmate was a constant talker, so it was hard to read. Now I read spy novels by R. Ludlum, *The Bourne Supremacy*, James Patterson. I've read twenty to twenty-five books in here. I prefer reference books, though, 'cause I like to learn more about antiques and collectibles, so I can build my knowledge."

In 1998, while doing time in Stanislaus County Jail for fraud, Gilkey said he had read John Dunning's *Booked to Die*, a novel in which a woman collector does copious research on rare books and profits from her knowledge. It was this book that had inspired Gilkey to become more serious, more thorough, with his own research about rare books.

Gilkey said that he didn't like to spend his "own money" on books, and that it wasn't fair that he didn't have enough money to afford all the rare books he wanted. For Gilkey, "fairness" seemed to be a synonym for "satisfaction": if he is satisfied, all is deemed fair; if not, it isn't. I had no idea how to respond, especially because of his unfailing equanimity while stating his views.

"I have a degree in economics," he said, in an effort to

explain his compulsion to steal. "I figure the more books I get for free, if I need to sell them, I get a hundred percent profit."

It took me a few seconds to realize that Gilkey was not joking. He was so calm and polite that statements like these were particularly jolting, bringing into sharp and unnerving focus his skewed sense of what is fair and right and reasonable. Back and forth, as though a pendulum were swinging in and out of his conscience, Gilkey alternated between claiming that he would never commit another crime, and presenting ideas of how to "get" more books. "I want to stop committing crime. It's not worth it," he said. Then, "There's the excitement of having the books in your hands." The conversation continued this way, swinging from his desire for books to his plan to quit stealing them. Only one of these wishes seemed genuine, or even possible.

Gilkey has been arrested several times for writing bad checks for books, which he told me he didn't know was against the law.

"I mean, I thought it was a civil issue, not a criminal one," he said.

I knew that this was as unlikely as the story he had just told me about how he got the children's book *Madeline.*

"I went to a flea market and I bought a first-edition *Madeline* by Ludwig Bemelmans for one dollar. It's worth fifteen hundred now."

Much of what he had said so far was true (Sanders had already given me some of the same information), but surely not all of it.

I turned our conversation to the 2003 book fair in San Francisco, where Sanders thought he had seen Gilkey, although I did not mention Sanders.

"Yeah, I went," he said, "but I think people knew about me."

He had just posted bail and brought with him to the fair a couple of books he had hoped to sell to unsuspecting dealers in order to raise money for an attorney. He had roamed up and down the aisles, chatting with dealers and admiring books and color plates from an Audubon folio. One of the books he carried around at the fair was, appropriately enough, *The Invisible Man.*

"But I got the feeling I was being watched," he said, "so I left."

So maybe Sanders was not, as his colleague suggested, paranoid. Maybe the man he had locked eyes with on the opening day of the fair was indeed Gilkey.

"But you know," said Gilkey, "the police never got me. That's not how I got caught. Some ABAA security chair got me. Ken something. I can't remember his last name."

He looked at me to see if I knew, but I did not want to appear to be on Sanders's side, so I said nothing. I had spent the last half-hour trying to parse Gilkey's truths from his lies, and now the half-truth of my silence lodged as its own kind of deception.

Gilkey started to tell me the names of other books he would like to collect, but stopped mid-sentence because a guard had signaled him. Our thirty minutes were up.

Driving home from hot, dry Tracy to cool, crisp San Francisco, I replayed my conversation with Gilkey in my head. He was not the flinty, belligerent criminal I had expected, nor had he been completely straight with me. What I felt sure of was that he was a man completely enthralled by books and how they might express his ideal self. He was a collector like other collectors—but also not like them. His polite manner had been a relief at first, but had become disconcerting. Reconciling the face of composure with his history of crime was no simple task, and it was about to become even more complicated.

## ❧ 3 ❧

# Richie Rich

When Gilkey was released from prison several weeks later, we met at Café Fresco in Union Square, his choice. It's up the street from Saks Fifth Avenue, where he used to work. The café's décor is faux Italian, with extra-large cans of tomatoes and bags of pasta gathering dust on metal shelves across from a refrigerated case of doughnuts that Hispanic women ring up at the register. It is as though someone thought the café should have the façade of Italian country charm, but abandoned the idea when it was half done.

Gilkey wore a pressed white shirt, a dark blue baseball cap with "PGA Golf" printed across it, and brand-new beige leather sneakers, the kind you don't usually see on anyone under sixty-five. The shirt and jacket once belonged to his father, who had died while Gilkey was doing time at DVI. He said he missed his father a lot, then pulled a crumpled tissue from the jacket pocket. "Huh," he said, looking at the tissue, "this was his," then put it back in his pocket. I picked up a cup of tea at the counter, and he ordered an orange juice and a doughnut, for which he thanked me profusely. We sat down at a table, and for two hours he answered my questions, most of which were of the straightforward who, what, where, when, and why variety, but it was this last question, *why*, more than any other, that had brought me there. Why did Gilkey love rare books? Why did he steal them? Why did he risk his freedom for them? And why was he willing to talk to me so frankly about it?

Before our meeting, I had read about where Gilkey grew up, hoping it might provide clues about the man and his motivations. He was born in 1968, in Modesto, California, a medium-sized town in rural San Joaquin Valley, which has since grown to nearly two hundred thousand people.[1] The first settlers arrived during the Gold Rush, their pockets empty and their heads filled with dreams of striking it rich, but like most immigrants drawn to California in the mid-1800s, most of them did not find their fortunes panning for gold. Over a hundred years later, Modesto developed into the idealized suburb popularized by native son George Lucas in *American Graffiti*. Today, the town solicits the television and film industries to use its "all-American" appearance as a backdrop.[2] Behind the fresh-scrubbed façade, however, is a town with one of the highest rates of car theft in the United States,[3] air quality that's often hazardous, and, according to 2007 statistics from the FBI, more rapes, violent crime, larceny, and property crime per capita than New York City. It is fitting that a man like Gilkey, intent on constructing his own false front, should have grown up in a place like Modesto, where the public image is so misleading.

Taking sips from his bottle of orange juice, Gilkey told me that he grew up the youngest in a family of eight. His father worked at Campbell's Soup Company as a transportation manager, and his mother was a housewife.

"My parents were just a normal couple, I guess. My mom's a homemaker. She loves to take care of children, take care of the house, that's all she likes to do. My father worked all the time. Eight to five, to bring in the money. My father did a lot of the gardening. My mom used to like to go to garage sales. Just regular stuff, I guess. Just regular family stuff."

When I asked Gilkey about when he started collecting books, he said, "I kept a collection of Richie Rich comic books in my bedroom."

Richie Rich was an odd-looking character who wore short pants and a large bow tie, but was a pleasant and likable boy from a family with bottomless wealth. The allure for kids was the fantasy of great riches and instant gratification. Richie Rich could get whatever he wanted with minimal effort. That

Gilkey, a man whose dream is to be wealthy and refined, would have collected not *Superman* or *X-Men* or *Fantastic Four* but *Richie Rich* seemed the kind of detail a B-movie writer might propose to a director. Gilkey seemed unaware of the irony as he explained the attraction.

"I liked the kid, wearing a bow tie . . . and the colorful cover. Nice stories, easy to read. He was so rich. [He was] just playing baseball with Pee Wee or Freckles, doing the things that kids do. But they were rich, they had vaults and all that, where all the money was, diamonds and jewelry, treasures. I guess everybody wants to be rich."

Maybe, but not everyone wants desperately for others to see him as rich. It was this aspect of Gilkey's collecting that set him apart from other collectors I had met and read about. For them, however gratifying it might be to have the admiration and envy of others, it is not the driving incentive of their collecting. There are, undoubtedly, those who collect to impress (Sanders likens them to African big-game hunters: "Take aim—boom—you've got a trophy!"), but I had the sense that it was usually secondary to other reasons. One collector I met was delighted to show me her extensive and varied book collection.[4] She had been gathering them for over a decade, but no one had ever asked to see them before. "None of my friends get it," she said. Her growing library was a private pleasure, pure and simple. Gilkey had other motivations, as his enthusiasm for Richie Rich indicated.

———

I wouldn't be able to name a single issue of a comic book I read as a child. Occasionally, I glanced at my older brother's issues of *MAD* or a friend's *Archie*s, but I was not interested in comics. I did collect, though. Huddled on my childhood shelves were glass animals, carnelian stones I had dug up at the beach, ceramic animals that came packed inside my mother's boxes of tea, and, for reasons that now escape me, the striped paper straws that Pixy Stix candy came in. The difference, however, between my desire to accumulate and the true collector's was that I added to each assemblage with mild pleasure, not fevered focus. The haphazard, infrequent expansion of my collections gave me a sense of constancy (another carnelian! bigger than the others, but *like* them) and confirmed identity (no one I knew collected these objects; it was *my* thing)—two common satisfactions of childhood. But eventually, after I'd amassed a couple dozen of each object, I would forget about them. I was easily sated, something probably no collector would say about himself. My only true passion as a child was an intense study of ballet, where what I collected were strained muscles, blisters, and, more than anything, a deep sense of purpose and joy. Throughout those years, I was drawn to classmates who were troublemakers, those who talked back to teachers and pulled off pranks that landed them in the principal's office. (I've heard that two of these kids ended up in prison.) I never dared disobey, but got a secret thrill from their doing so. Being around Gilkey was similarly exciting, although instead of the visceral thrill I remember having as a kid, it was an intellectual one. I couldn't fathom what it was about books that made him continually risk jail time for them.

Going over Gilkey's childhood seemed to be a good way to begin satisfying my curiosity. He told me that one afternoon when he was around nine or ten, he climbed into the family station wagon with his parents and sister Tina, and headed toward downtown Modesto, to Montgomery Ward, where he was about to commit his first crime. Wandering through the department store, he admired the thirty-nine-cent Hot Wheels cars and action figures like Superman and The Incredible Hulk, but kept browsing. No one in his family was looking when he picked up a catcher's mitt, and they didn't notice it on the way out. Once outside the store, he held up his prize.

"Look what I just did," he said.

They looked, said nothing, and continued walking through the lines of cars in the parking lot. When they got home, Gilkey, a right-handed boy, realized that the catcher's mitt he had just swiped was a lefty.

When I asked Gilkey why his parents hadn't punished him, he shrugged.

"I wasn't surprised they didn't say anything," he said. "I'd just get in more trouble if I returned it."

I couldn't let this one go, but when I asked further questions about it, Gilkey seemed puzzled by my insistent probing. Maybe the memory, like most family legends, had taken on its own kind of logic over the years. For him, there was no mystery to it. Still, telling me about snatching the mitt seemed to have jogged similar memories, because Gilkey was off and running. He told me that his family had a penchant for stealing from one another. He claimed his sister and brother had stolen some of his books while he was in prison. He said he and one of his brothers stole from a sister when they were helping her move from one apartment to another. He claimed that another sister and brother had both stolen from their mother's belongings. Apparently, this familial filching was going on even a generation before.

"My father's mom collected books," said Gilkey. "She gave him the books, but his sister stole some."

I returned to the main subject I was there to learn about: Gilkey's book collecting. When I asked if his parents had collected, he said that at an early age he learned from them that seemingly worthless objects could grow in value, so if you could get them cheaply, all the better.

"I used to go to garage sales when I was younger and wait in the car with my dad. I didn't really care about them, but then my parents would come back with stories. 'Look what I got for a quarter, and I bet it's worth seventy or eighty dollars. . . . They're just giving it away!'"

They brought home their finds and set them on shelves or in boxes, along with the rest of their beloved collected objects, and waited for their value to climb.[5]

At DVI, Gilkey had told me that his family owned thousands of books, and now he remembered some of his favorites, "a couple of leather-bound Time-Life books, especially the Western series." He said, again with no apparent awareness of irony, that another favorite, *Crimes and Punishment*, an illustrated crime encyclopedia not to be confused with Dostoyevsky's *Crime and Punishment*, still stands on the shelves, whereas a set of one hundred law books his parents bought do not. "We took them off the shelf to make space for other books," he said.

"If you have a bookcase," added Gilkey, "the more you put on them, the more it builds up, the more it's worth, the better it looks. . . . With books, it looks beautiful, you can read it if you want, and it's part of the ambience of a house, isn't it? And it will go up in value. Shouldn't every house have a bookcase? It's just the pleasure of . . . Say you have somebody who's never seen you before, and you take them in and say, 'Here's my library.'"[6]

*Here's my library?* I had always thought of my books as fairly private things, not for display, but the ability to show them off seemed crucial to Gilkey. Then again, a wall in my living room is covered with bookshelves, and everyone who visits can see what I have read. If I am honest with myself, I must admit that to some degree my books are badges: there's the faded spine of James Joyce's *Ulysses* (willing to persevere! it shouts), Carlos Fuentes's *Terra Nostra* (she doesn't just read Americans and Europeans!), Virginia Woolf's *A Room of One's Own* (look, a feminist classic!), etc. So, was the difference between my interest and appreciation of books and Gilkey's only a matter of degree? There must be more to it than that. And what about the criminal side of his collecting? When I asked him about it, Gilkey told me how his use of credit card fraud began.

Sometime in 1996, according to Gilkey, he was with a friend at the Red Lion Doubletree Inn in Modesto. "I found a credit card receipt on the floor," he said. "I told him I was going to see if I could charge a few things using the number, but he said it would never work. A couple hours later, using the hotel pay phone, I got a bunch of stuff: a watch, a pizza, and a poster of the movie *Psycho*."

Gilkey got away with these thefts because he had not stolen the credit card itself, in which case the card's owner could have alerted authorities and canceled all charges. Instead, by using the number off a receipt, its owner wouldn't hear about the charge until the next bill. In the end, it was the retailer who would get stiffed. Even when the retailer has insurance, book dealers later told me, the deductible is often considerable, sometimes equaling what was stolen.

The "friend" whom Gilkey mentioned as his accomplice was likely his own father, whom he had already told me he always hung around with. He went on to describe his fraudulent purchases as though they were larks, why-the-hell-not pranks, but the ease with which he pulled them off stuck with him. "It was that easy," he said, a phrase that he would repeat almost every time he told a story of book theft. At the time, he was working at the Modesto Post Office, for $11 an hour.

"That was enough money for some things," said Gilkey, "but not enough for books."

✤ ✤

SOMETHING TOLD ME that for Gilkey, no matter how much money he had, it would never be enough for all the books he craved. Sigmund Freud described collecting antiquities as "second only in intensity to his nicotine addiction."[7] He explained that the drive and pleasure in any kind of collecting comes from the sense of conquest. "I am by nature nothing but a conquistador," he wrote, "an adventurer, if you wish to translate the term, with all the inquisitiveness, daring and tenacity capable of such a man."[8]

The difference between a person who appreciates books, even loves them, and a collector is not only degrees of affection, I realized. For the former, the bookshelf is a kind of memoir: there are my childhood books, my college books, my favorite novels, my inexplicable choices. Many matchmaking and social networking websites offer a place for members to list what they're reading for just this reason: books can reveal a lot about a person. This is particularly true of the collector, for whom the bookshelf is a reflection not just of what he has read but profoundly of who he is: "Ownership is the most intimate relationship that one can have to objects. Not that they can come alive in him; it is he who comes alive in them," wrote cultural critic Walter Benjamin.[9]

❖ ❖

GILKEY CAME ALIVE in this way in the spring of 1997 when he went to his first antiquarian book fair. He told me he had recently lost his job as a mail sorter at the post office, and his father had left his mother. Father and son, now as inseparable as favorite brothers, went to Los Angeles, where they were thinking about renting a place together. One morning, while reading the *Los Angeles Times*, Gilkey noticed an advertisement for a book fair in Burbank and decided to check it out.

Wandering through the fair, he was impressed by the number of dealers. His plan was to find some good books and to "get" about a thousand dollars' worth of them. He was in awe of the collections. *I could own those*, he thought. Having recently attended the book fair in New York, I understood his awe. Being among such ravishing books, and so many of them, is intoxicating enough for the average book lover—but for Gilkey, it was an important, memorable high. The experience increased not only his appetite but his confidence in his ability to get what he wanted, how he wanted. He spotted a room where dealers specialized in horror books, one of his favorite genres, and selected three first editions: *The Dunwich Horror*, by H. P. Lovecraft, Ira Levin's *Rosemary's Baby*, and Isak Dinesen's *Seven Gothic Tales*. He "paid" for the books with bad checks and a maxed-out credit card.

Gilkey figured it was a matter of getting in and out fast, before anyone could figure out what he was up to. He was successful. Along with books, he picked up a copy of *Firsts*, a magazine about book collecting. Later, flipping through it, he came upon an advertisement for Bauman Rare Book Shop, which appeared to have "some very nice books" for sale. He called and asked them to send him a catalog, which arrived in a couple of days.

Gilkey described how he leafed through the catalog and began to seriously consider what it would be like to own a collection of books like those on its pages. He called Bauman again and asked for book recommendations. They mentioned a first-edition *Lolita*, a title he recognized. They explained that the book came with a green octavo shell (a protective box that's a common accessory for rare books). Gilkey had never heard of such a thing, but he liked the way it sounded. Plus, he thought, it wasn't that expensive for a book of its type, about $2,500. He placed the order, and *Lolita* arrived in two or three days.

Before, Gilkey had managed to acquire several collectible books, but this was the first one he regarded as truly valuable, not only because of its price (the other books Gilkey had picked up were under $1,000 each) but also because of its historical significance, its notoriety. *Lolita*, Vladimir Nabokov's provocative story of a middle-aged man's lust for a young girl, was first published in Paris in 1955 and has ranked high on banned-book lists ever since. In 1959, the author inscribed a copy to fellow novelist Graham Greene, "For Graham Greene from Vladimir Nabokov,

November 8, 1959." An accomplished lepidopterist, Nabokov also drew a delicate sketch of a butterfly, labeling it with what might be the most lyrical of inscriptions, "green swallowtail dancing waisthigh." As an association copy (one that an author gives, often with an inscription, to someone of particular interest), over time its value soared. At a Christie's auction in 2002, Greene's copy sold for $264,000.[10]

Although Gilkey's copy was worth a fraction of that, as his first valuable book, it held a special place in his heart. He put it on top of his piano and admired it. He liked the feel of the clamshell box it arrived in, how it was covered with a soft, textured fabric. He wished all covers were like that. The book was published in two volumes, in spring green wrappers (paper covers), with "Nabokov" printed on the top edges, "Lolita" in the middle, and "The Olympia Press" at the bottom edge. It was a simple design, elegant. Unlike the other books he had collected, he read *Lolita*, but found it "disgusting." I sensed that he told me this in order to win my respect—he may be a criminal, but he has morals. His disgust with the story of *Lolita*, however, did not affect his feelings about the book, because he was looking forward to its value increasing over time. This was not because he had any intention of selling it, but rather because it would give his collection greater status. Also, it was number four on the

Modern Library's list of the one hundred best English-language novels of the twentieth century.[14] He had just started reading and collecting books from this list, which he came across while researching rare books, and had decided that he wanted them all.

Gilkey added that he had used his own American Express card to buy *Lolita*, but I hadn't asked.

A few months after *Lolita* arrived, Gilkey and his father were staying at a hotel in Beverly Hills when he decided to use bad checks from the same checkbooks he had used at the Burbank book fair, this time to purchase foreign currency. He was arrested and put in jail for forty days, then sent back to Modesto under house arrest, during which time he wore an electronic ankle bracelet.

About a year later, on New Year's Eve 1998, he wrote another bad check to cover gambling losses at a casino. Again he was arrested.

"I just wanted some extra change, and I lost," he said, as though this might be a satisfactory explanation.

Gilkey didn't get out of prison until October 1999. When he did, he was feeling cheated and ready to be paid back. It was a cycle he would run through repeatedly: being sure he will never be caught, being arrested, doing time, then being released with a sense of entitlement and an eagerness for revenge that set him back on the same cycle. Having spent so many months behind bars, he felt as though he were running out of time.

"Once you've done time, you start to feel that way," he said. So he made a promise to himself and his aging father, who was almost eighty.

"I'm going to build us a grand estate."

## ❖ 4 ❖

# A Gold Mine

When, at the start of 1999, Ken Sanders received a letter from the Antiquarian Booksellers' Association of America asking him to vote on whether to dissolve the southwest chapter to which he belonged, it was out of pure orneriness that he voted against the change.[1] With only seventeen members, it was one of the smallest, and unlike larger chapters, it didn't hold fairs or meetings. Soon he discovered that he was the only member who had voted against dissolution, and although the votes in favor were enough to shut it down, the board decided otherwise. And since every chapter needs a representative and a president, they asked Sanders which position he would prefer to fill—a fair request, he thought, given his vote.

"I don't care—as long as it doesn't have to do with money," said Sanders, who has had financial problems for much of his life. "Whatever you do, don't make me treasurer."

He began his term as representative.

"The next thing I know I'm supposed to be at the board of governors' meeting in New York City. What the hell is that?!" said Sanders. He found out on the seventeenth floor of a Rockefeller Center building at his first board meeting, where they put him on a membership committee. Shortly thereafter, they also assigned him the position of security chair, about which he knew nothing.

A few weeks later, sitting at his desk, perched in a loft overlooking his store, Sanders got a call from the secretary in the ABAA's New York office.

"Have you vetted the pink sheets yet?" she asked.

"What pink sheets?" said Sanders.

He hadn't opened the box she sent him, assuming it was full of reference materials. When he pried it open, he uncovered a problem much bigger than abandoned pink sheets, the term for theft reports sent by dealers.

Since 1949, the ABAA has worked to promote and maintain ethical standards within the trade. There are now 455 bookseller members, and to join, each of them has to have been in business for at least four years, undergone intense scrutiny, and been recommended by ABAA members.[2] Until Sanders started working as security chair, when someone stole books from an ABAA dealer, that dealer would fill out a pink sheet and mail it to ABAA headquarters in New York. There, copies would be sent out with the next mass mailing, whenever it happened to come about, so that all members could be on the lookout for the stolen books. This would take considerably longer than the time it would take a thief to saunter out the door of one bookstore with a first edition of Kurt Vonnegut's *Slaughterhouse-Five*, for example, tucked into his coat and into the door of another, where he could sell it and walk away with several thousand dollars (depending on its condition, whether or not it's inscribed, has an original dust wrapper, etc., it's valued at up to $6,500). The box of pink sheets Sanders had inherited contained some that were over a year old but had not yet been distributed. He knew that at that point it was probably too late to send them out to dealers around the country.

*What the hell good is this doing anybody?* thought Sanders. The job hadn't come with instructions, and he knew little about technological options. "You know that scene from Kubrick's *2001* where the apes are grunting around the black monolith?" Sanders likes to say. "That's me and my computer every morning, seeing if it will work."

But he wanted to find a way to broadcast news of thefts immediately. First, he started using a private ABAA online discussion list to reach members. Then he campaigned the board of governors, declaring with characteristic zealousness, "I'm the security chair, dammit, I want a security line! I want a way to contact everyone, and since over half the membership doesn't subscribe to the discuss list, I need something else!" So although Sanders calls himself "a Luddite in cyberspace," he convinced the Internet committee to create a stolen-book database and an e-mail system to alert the hundreds of members of the ABAA and, soon thereafter, members of the International League of Antiquarian Booksellers (ILAB), which includes two thousand booksellers in thirty countries.

In November, about six months after the e-mail system had been set up, John Gilkey was reading the *San Francisco Chronicle* when an advertisement caught his attention: Saks Fifth Avenue was hiring salespeople. The next day, he dressed in a shirt, tie, and slacks from a too-tight pin-striped suit, and took the ninety-mile train ride from Modesto to San Francisco.

Saks Men's Store sits just outside the center of Union Square, on a block with glittering sidewalks and neighbors like Armani, Burberry, and Cartier. It is a high-rent district that attracts big spenders, something that Gilkey found attractive. He figured that by working in a place like Saks, he would come in contact with wealthy clientele, "no riffraff." He also assumed that since it was a quality place specializing in luxury goods, he would get paid more, maybe even earn commissions and discounts. He was right on all counts. (Saks declined my repeated requests to respond to Gilkey's claims.)

Saks would turn out to be an almost ideal working environment for Gilkey, offering him opportunities to speak with people who belonged to a world he desperately wanted to be a part of. *Almost* ideal, however, because while these people had money, they weren't necessarily well educated or in possession of large libraries, as he knew he would be, given the same means.

Sitting in the Saks employment office, Gilkey completed the application, noting his brief experience working at a Robinson-May department store in Los Angeles. He must have seemed perfect for the job: polite, experienced, and not too badly dressed. Where they asked for his name, he neatly filled it in, but when he reached the part of the application where he was supposed to write whether he had ever been convicted of a crime, he left it blank.

He was asked to start the next day.

❖ ❖

WHENEVER I HAVE ASKED Gilkey to describe the allure books have for him, he struggles, but ultimately settles on the aesthetic. "It's a visual thing, the way they look, all lined up on the shelf." He once suggested an almost sexual attraction to books. "I don't know. Maybe it's because I'm a man, but I like to look."

As Patricia Hampl wrote in a book about beauty's bewitching qualities: "Collecting is not a simple matter of possessing. It's a way of looking: a looking that is itself a kind of craving. To look this way is to be possessed, lost."[3]

Collectors talking about the books they have just acquired, or the ones they haven't been able to get their hands on, or those snatched away by another collector, sound a lot like lotharios reminiscing about lovers. At a San Francisco book fair, Peter Stern, a gray-haired Boston dealer clad in a tweed jacket, with a plaid scarf around his neck, said he doesn't collect anymore, but occasionally a book will catch his eye. When this happens, "I ache to buy it. I want it desperately."[4] But acquiring the object of his affection changes everything. "The moment I own it, even if it's for a few seconds, that's enough. I could sell it the next minute, and I don't even remember it sometimes. I'm looking forward to the next book."

It is not uncommon to read pronouncements from besotted collectors that make the "mania" in "bibliomania" seem an understatement. "Too few people seem to realize that books have feelings," wrote collector Eugene Field, who wrote *The Love Affairs of a Bibliomaniac* in 1896. "But if I know one thing better than another I know this, that my books know me and love me. When of a morning I awaken I cast my eyes about my room to see how fare my beloved treasures, and as I cry cheerily to them, 'Good-day to you, sweet friends!' how lovingly they beam upon me, and how glad they are that my repose has been unbroken."[5]

❖ ❖

AT SAKS, Gilkey was in a world of tasteful luxury. He had been assigned to work in the Men's Store on the first floor, in "men's furnishings," where meticulously folded garments of fine cottons, silks, and wools sat in floor-to-ceiling glass-fronted wood cabinetry. He would start his day checking the floor, clearing away any detritus left by the previous day's shoppers. He would stroll past hand-stitched Borrelli shirts (starting around $350) and Etro ties ($130 and up), and chat with fellow workers. Because it was the holidays, when Saks customers can't seem to get enough luxury goods, the floor was usually packed. They needed extra help, "floaters," to work in various departments, which is why Gilkey was hired. He enjoyed the job and took special pleasure in spying local socialites and celebrities, such as Ann Getty and Sharon Stone, who was then married to *San Francisco Chronicle* editor Phil Bronstein. Gilkey prided himself on being a good employee, always on time. He was friendly and thought that everyone at Saks, "especially the people in the loss prevention department," were nice to him. He had snowed even the watchdogs, and I could imagine how. His decorous way of speaking, deferential affect, and calm demeanor would be valuable assets on the sales floor, where big spenders would be accustomed to being treated with such regard.

In addition to consulting Gilkey about their purchases, customers sometimes asked to open instant credit accounts. He would dutifully take down their information—names, numbers, addresses, and so on—and when they would tell him that they needed higher credit limits, he would call the business office and communicate their requests. When the office checked a customer's credit rating and decided to grant a more generous limit, increasing it from, say, $4,000 to $8,000, Gilkey noticed.

This was a part-time job, only two or three days a week, but even if Gilkey had been working full-time, his salary would never have afforded him what he wanted. One day, while he was opening a new account for a customer, he realized what he held in his hands. *A gold mine,* he thought. Whenever he opened the instant accounts, he could put the audit copy in his pocket, go out to lunch, and write the information on a separate piece of paper, which he could refer to later when placing orders over the phone. That day at lunch, he did just that. He walked down the street to the Westin Hotel, took the elevator to the second-floor lobby, which offered some degree of privacy, and wrote down the credit card numbers listed on the instant account. The next day, he did it again. So it went, through the holidays. He was careful not to take every account record, however, hoping to avoid raising suspicions.

It was not long before Gilkey realized that he had yet another source for credit card information. In those days, customers' entire credit card numbers were printed on receipts. Each receipt included a copy for the customer and a copy for the auditing department at Saks. Salespeople were asked to cross out the number on the customers' copies, but the audit copies remained fully intact. According to Gilkey, when salespeople were rushed, they sometimes threw away copies, so even if, from time to time, he were to forget to turn one in, it would not be noticed.

Gilkey didn't use the information to buy anything right away. He needed to wait enough time so that customers notified of fraudulent activity wouldn't trace the last use of their cards back to Saks. He would save the account numbers for a rainy day. Holding off spending, he harvested five to ten receipts a week.

# ✤ 5 ✤

# Spider-Man

K en Sanders Rare Books is located on the edge of down-town Salt Lake City in a four-thousand-square-foot former tire shop endowed with high ceilings and abundant sunlight. The store is chockablock with so much old, beautiful, and bizarre printed matter—books, photographs, broadsides, postcards, pamphlets, maps—that a quick in-and-out trip takes more willpower than the average book lover can summon. The first time I visited, Sanders, dressed in jeans and a Hawaiian shirt, showed me around.

Standing near the entrance, he gestured toward a room to the left, where he keeps the rarest of his books. Although he is not religious, many of these are Mormon texts. This is Utah, after all, where demand for such books is high, and as he reminded me, he needs to make a living. Next, he directed my attention to the glass case separating the rare book room from those who might be inclined to tuck a nice little volume into the waistband of their pants (a common hiding place for book thieves). Inside the case were several books he loves: first editions of Ginsberg, Burroughs, Ferlinghetti, and Kerouac, in a display Sanders had set up the week before for the fiftieth anniversary of the publication of Ginsberg's *Howl*.

Sanders led me to the main part of the store. In addition to more than a hundred thousand books and other materials ("If it's printed, it's here"), there are busts of Mark Twain and Demosthenes, cardboard cutouts of R. Crumb characters, and headless mannequins modeling T-shirts printed with characters from Edward Abbey's *The Monkey Wrench Gang*. The store reflects much of what Sanders cares about—books by Wallace Stegner, Edward Abbey, and B. Traven; music from the sixties; radical politics; the environment; and beautiful graphics. But of all that he cares about, it's clear that his children are at the top of the list. Sometimes, Sanders's daughter, Melissa, who used to work in the store, visits from California and lends a hand. When Melissa and her brother, Michael, were young, Sanders's marriage fell apart and he took over their rearing himself.

"To have that kind of anchor . . . They probably saved my own sanity at certain points in my life," he said. "It's not easy for any single parent to raise children, whether it's a mom or dad, it's just more unusual for it to be the father. I have no regrets. I probably raised them like wild wolves, but I did the best I could. Melissa still remembers the summer I dragged them through Death Valley when it was a hundred and thirty-seven degrees. I made them get out of the car and walk in the sand dunes. 'Dad tried to kill my brother and me,' she says."

Sanders will tell me this story several times, always with a proud and mischievous grin.

Next to the counter sat a gathering of armchairs and a few red plastic glasses left over from the evening before. At about five P.M. every day, Sanders offers wine, bourbon, and beer from a small fridge next to the counter to friends who drop by. One of those friends, "Captain Eddie," digital artist Edward Bateman, told me that the bookstore is the nexus of Salt Lake City's counterculture. I could see why. Sanders's store has the appeal of an eccentric great-aunt's attic, where in every corner you might just happen upon treasure. Add to that his raconteur's charm, and it's no wonder the store is a favored gathering spot. With the hum of slow-moving fans in the background, writers, authors, artists, and filmmakers sip and reminisce about recent readings in the store, the best of them raucous literary happenings, while Sanders starts planning the next one. Around them, the R. Crumb characters, the busts, and the faces of the Monkey Wrench Gang seem like ghostly participants in the conversation. On the wall behind the counter hangs a large portrait of Sanders that a friend of his painted. "I call it my Dorian Gray," he says. "I've always wanted to get those Disney eyes for it—to watch the store."

The store could use them. Before my visit, during our first phone conversation, Sanders had mentioned the Red Jaguar Guy, and during the tour, when I asked for details, he gave me a look that said, *Are you ready for this?* I had already heard enough of Sanders's stories to know that I'd opened the door to a good one, and nothing seems to make him happier than finding a willing ear for his tales.

"It's actually an embarrassing story. For six years I've been leading the charge against theft—how booksellers can protect themselves from credit card fraud—and this punk-ass kid in his twenties gets me. 'Ryan' comes into the store and tells me that he and his father are selling books online and being real successful at it. Over the next week or so he buys some copies of the *Book of Mormon*, some other books. Makes three purchases totaling five thousand five hundred dollars, and each time the credit card company approved the charge. Then I get a call from another Salt Lake City bookseller who complained to me that he had just received a chargeback for a *Book of Mormon* sale a month back. I was curious and walked over to his shop. The individual he described to me matched the description of Ryan. I began to get a sinking feeling. I called other shops and found that Ryan had been to at least two of them. So I called the credit card company, and they did nothing, those *swine.* I began alerting every book dealer from Provo to Logan and discovered that there were five of us who had been visited by Ryan. I then received a phone call from a Provo dealer who had seen one of my stolen copies of the *Book of Mormon* on eBay (an 1874 edition). Thinking I had found my thief, I called up the seller, who turned out to be an elderly man named Fred who mainly sold low-end books on eBay—and I put the fear of God into him. Fred says, 'I didn't steal your books, but I know Ryan.' Says he meets him in parking lots and pays cash."

Sanders coerced Fred into arranging a rendezvous with Ryan, then Sanders called the police. "Ryan agrees to meet Fred at three in the Smith's grocery store parking lot," explained Sanders. "Ryan says, 'I'll be driving a red Jag.' I called the cops, who didn't give a shit. They say to me, 'Who are you? Why'd you call?' Just try to find a cop who cares about stolen books. I tell him I've pieced it together: five booksellers, fifteen grand. I tell him, 'If you're not going to do anything about this, I'll go over and take him down myself.' So the cop came to my shop and reluctantly agreed to set up the sting, with the admonishment that I stay away."

Ambivalence is not in Sanders's emotional vocabulary,

and his storytelling engine was revved up, rolling forward in full fury.

"Fred calls me and says the cops just showed up in the black-and-whites and scared the shit out of Ryan—then he says, 'Wait, he's runnin' away!' So I get there as fast as I can and see—oh, I tell you, it was a *beautiful* sight—a brand-new red Jaguar from Hertz with its doors wide open." Sanders leans forward and takes a quick breath. "There's this kid in a squad car with his head in his hands, bawling. The officer says to him, 'You know who this is?' And the kid looks up at me with this look, like, *Oh no, I'm doomed.* Then, get this: the cops *forget* about me. They leave the doors wide open, and here's this kid, so I get in his face and say, 'WHERE THE HELL ARE MY BOOKS?!' He tells me there's this drug ring. Fourteen others involved. I tell you, he was scared. This kid was really scared, because he knows they'll come after him. So the next day I call the cops to see what's going on and they tell me they tried questioning him this morning, but he wants an attorney. I couldn't believe it! Why didn't they question him while he was scared? Why did they wait?" Sanders finally pauses to take a deep breath. "So, anyway, this morning, I get a call. It's been six months since they questioned him. Turns out the kid's from a well-to-do family. He was allowed to promise to go into drug rehab in exchange for not serving any time."

Sanders ended this story the way he ends a lot of stories

about book thieves. "Nothing—I'm telling you, *nothing*— ever happens to these guys."

It's a wonder Sanders's business has been successful for so many years (he reports sales of $1.9 million in 2007), considering many of the decisions he makes. His devotion to fellow book lovers, for example, usually trumps any chance of profit. About midway through my tour of his store, he noticed a customer at the counter. The man had a copy of *History of the Scofield Mine Disaster*, by J. W. Dilley, published in 1900, which chronicles Utah's most horrific mining catastrophe. The man said that his grandfather had been one of the few survivors. Sanders took the book from him and flipped open the cover: $500.

"You don't want this," he said, shutting the book. "I've got another copy, much cheaper, I'm sure." He turned to his employee, Mike Nelson, and said, "Go look for another copy in the back."

Mike said he was pretty sure that that was the only copy, but Sanders insisted. When Mike returned several minutes later, having dug up a very beat-up copy, Sanders handed it to the man.

"See?" he said, visibly pleased with himself. "Only eighty dollars—and the bonus is that it looks like it survived the fire!"

How Sanders determines whether a book is worth $500 or $80 is based on several factors.

"In fields that I know something about and the few that I have some expertise in, experience weighs heavily on my decisions to acquire certain books or collections," he wrote in a lengthy e-mail to me, "and ultimately that experience and knowledge will determine how I price the item."

Much of a book's value depends on literary fashion, and tastes change. Supply and demand also affect value. The first printing of Hemingway's *In Our Time*, for example, was very small (1,225 copies), in contrast to the fifty-thousand-copy print run of *The Old Man and the Sea*. Pricing reflects that. Further factors include whether there's a dust jacket (if not, the value is negligible), and if those jackets are price-clipped, worn, torn, or soiled. Modern first editions in poor shape can be worth as little as ten percent of a "perfect" copy.

So one copy of *History of the Scofield Mine Disaster* can be less than a fifth of the price of another—in this case, due to condition. The $80 price was undoubtedly fair, but I noticed that when Mike, who was well aware of what Sanders refers to as "their cash flow challenges," heard Sanders announce the price of the bedraggled copy, he slumped at his desk behind the counter.

❖ ❖

BORN IN 1951, Ken Sanders was raised in a lapsed Mormon household in deeply devout Salt Lake City. He was encouraged to read and to collect, as his father did. (The elder Sanders, who passed away in 2008, built the preeminent collection of bottles manufactured in Utah, housed in a garage-museum next to his house.) Early on, Sanders began to view the Mormon social landscape with a fair amount of skepticism and the natural landscape with a reverence rivaled only by his love of books. Surrounded by believers at school and in the community, he said he learned "just enough about religion to stay the hell away from it." It would not be stretching matters, however, to say that from the start, reading was his faith.

"My dad joked that when my mom gave birth to me I was clutching a book," he said. As a boy, he devoured every book the librarians let him get his hands on, and some they didn't. Once, on a school field trip to the South Salt Lake Library, he tried to check out copies of *Dracula* and *Frankenstein*, but because they were from the adult section, the librarian refused. He found a way to read them anyway. As much as he enjoyed withdrawing books from the library, though, he preferred owning them. At Woodrow Wilson Elementary, he lived for the Scholastic Book Service and Weekly Reader Books. "They would cost twenty-five, thirty-five cents. I'd recycle pop bottles for a nickel apiece and save up. Once a month, teachers would collect orders. Then the box would come, and the teacher would call out names and hand out a book here, a couple of books there. I was always the last kid called because there was always an entire box for me. I had more books ordered than the rest of the class put together. Such great classics as *The Shy Stegasaurus of Cricket Creek*. Oh, I loved that one." To this day, he keeps at least one copy of it and other childhood favorites like *Danny Dunn and the Antigravity Paint* and *Mrs. Pickerell Goes to Mars* stocked in his store.

In junior high, Sanders was still a stubborn, determined boy who did what he needed to get what he wanted, even if it meant going up against formidable forces. It was a trait that he would make ample use of as security chair of the ABAA. On Saturdays Sanders would head downtown, walking all five miles instead of taking the bus in order to save money. With extra change in his pocket, he would try to muster courage for what he was about to do. Back then, he was desperate to get his hands on more comic books, but to do so he had to brave the surly junk store owner, who seemed to take pleasure in taunting kids.

"I was afraid of that old man," he said. "If you went in, he'd yell at ya, but I wanted those comic books so bad. I'd go in and hang my belly over the lard barrel and reach down in there and fish out those forties and fifties comic books, then go up to the counter shaking, the man yelling at me all the time. He was probably just pulling my leg, but I was too young to know it."

Soon after Sanders started collecting old comic books, he discovered Spider-Man. "The guy had problems," he said, describing the superhero's allure. "He had powers, but he was messed up. What awkward kid wouldn't be attracted to that?" In contrast, Superman was invincible and boring. Spider-Man was a questioning, rebellious guy who knew he was doing right, but the world was hostile and suspicious of him. Years later, toward the end of Sanders's term as security chair for the ABAA, one of his friends, a fellow bookseller, would describe him as "an outlaw who for the past six years has been *the* law."

When he was fourteen, Sanders's grandparents, Pop and Grammy, took him on a trip that would set the course of his life. They took him and his brother Doug to Southern California, where they visited Disneyland and Knott's Berry Farm, and the one place Sanders had requested specially: Bertrand Smith's Acres of Books. "I have no idea how I ever heard about them in the first place, but I still remember the address: 240 Long Beach Boulevard, Long Beach, California.

It was a really hot, hot day. Pop and I drove through the ship-yards in Long Beach in a 1950s Ford Sedan. He parked right in front of the store. I was in there for hours, and the whole time, he just sat there in the car, chain-smoking the unfil-tered Camels he would one day die from."

There's a difference between those who simply love books and those who collect them, and an experienced dealer can spot a collector in the time it takes to ask where they've stashed the first edition of *The Hobbit* (not likely to be sitting on open shelves). Bertrand Smith's heart must have skipped a beat when young Sanders strolled in, eyes wide.

"The store went on seemingly to infinity," said Sanders. "Stacks and stacks, tangled and overgrown, like a deep dark forest, but instead of trees, there were books. You had to climb up a rickety ladder to get to them, and it was hard to see because the only light in the place came from skylights way, way up. There was a locked room to the left where the rare books were. Bertrand Smith was a crusty old man, but somehow, I worked up the courage to ask him about my passions: Lewis Carroll, Edgar Allan Poe, Maxfield Parrish. He actually let me into the rare book room, where I sat at the table, leafing through Poe's *The Raven*. Each quatrain of the poem got a ten-by-fourteen-inch engraving by the nineteenth-century French illustrator Gustave Doré. I was thrilled. I remember it vividly—two feet tall and sixteen inches across, for seventeen dollars and fifty cents. I also bought a Maxfield Parrish, *The Arabian Nights*, for a few dollars, and an *Alice in Wonderland*, illustrated by Gwynedd Hudson, for two-fifty. She illustrated only two books in her life, and still, it's one of my favorites. I had been putting coins in the piggy bank at Pop and Grammy's, and Grammy had matched my deposits. I spent every blessed nickel I had on books that day. Still do. I'm older, balder, fatter, but not necessarily wiser."

In 1975, Sanders and a couple of friends took over a hippie head shop called the Cosmic Aeroplane in Salt Lake City, moved it to a new location, and began selling books. Among those looking for cheap paperbacks were budding collectors. Sanders went about stocking his shelves for them while listening to his favorite tunes, like the Electric Prunes' "I Had Too Much to Dream Last Night." The store was a huge success. At its height, according to Sanders, he and his two partners were pulling in $1.4 million a year in sales and had thirty employees. But the store was not without its struggles.

"The Cosmic Aeroplane was big and sprawling, and shoplifting was a constant problem," said Sanders. "The most memorable case involved the wife of an old friend. She began by selling me her knitting-book collection. She'd bring in a bag of books every week or so, then with more frequency and increasing quantity. The funny thing was, the books started getting newer and newer, until it became painfully obvious that she was stealing them from somewhere."

Sanders sighed. His telling of this story lacked the vigor of others. This woman may have been a thief, but she was also a friend, and the awkwardness of the situation, even twenty-five years later, seemed no less painful to him.

"We began by assigning someone to watch her every time she set foot in the store. The knitting bag she used to transport the books she wished to sell turned out to be full of books again by the time she was done browsing and left the store. Only thing was, the books were all stolen from us. I called around to the King's English and Sam Weller's bookstores and discovered that she was a regular at those shops as well. I read off a list of the most recently purchased titles from her to both stores, and, of course, they both had copies missing from their new-book inventories. Next time she came in I called the police and had them waiting outside the shop. When she departed with her knitting bag full of books, I had her arrested."

The knitting thief was one of a few success stories. Most thieves were never caught, and the anger and frustration they caused Sanders seems never to have completely subsided.

In 1981, the year Sanders left the Cosmic Aeroplane, he

would commit his own crime, although it was for a noble cause. Edward Abbey, author of *The Monkey Wrench Gang*, *Desert Solitaire*, and *The Fool's Progress*, had become a friend of Sanders, "in spite of my telling him I didn't think that Hayduke [protagonist of *The Monkey Wrench Gang*] should go around littering the countryside with beer cans. He quietly listened, but I don't think he gave a shit. One day, he called me, which he almost never did because he hated telephones, and said in his gruff voice, 'I'm going to be conducting spring rites at Glen Canyon Dam. If you want to talk [about a publishing project Sanders had proposed], meet me there.'"

When Sanders arrived, Abbey and a few friends were preparing to drop a three-hundred-foot tapered sheet of black plastic over the edge of Glen Canyon, a symbolic crack in the dam. It was the first national public event for the radical environmental group Earth First! Abbey, Sanders, and the rest of the group escaped arrest for trespassing and left with their appetites whetted for more pranks that might open the public's eyes to what they considered crimes against the environment.

Sanders had started Dream Garden Press, and in the following few years published Western wilderness calendars with excerpts of Abbey's writing, the R. Crumb illustrated edition of *The Monkey Wrench Gang*, and a couple of other

projects. He invited Abbey and Crumb to Utah for book sign-
ings. One of his favorite stories from this time took place at
a university bookstore.

"I had a car full of cartons of books. Two hundred people
were standing in line for autographs. There were Crumb and
Abbey, dutifully scribbling their names. One guy walks up to
Crumb and says, 'Mr. Abbey?' And Crumb, before he answers, looks over at Abbey, and they exchange this glance.
Crumb looks back to the guy and says, 'Yes?' And he signs
that copy of the book 'Edward Abbey'! Then he passed it to
Abbey, who signed it 'R. Crumb'! I would kill for that copy,"
said Sanders. "I'm sure that to this day, that guy doesn't
know of the deception. I keep praying that someday that
book will wander in here. I've been searching for it for
twenty years."

Later, because of disagreements with his partners, Sanders
left the Cosmic Aeroplane. This was the same period that his
marriage split, and alone he began raising Michael, age nine,
and Melissa, age seven.

Sanders kept his family going with a small office and a
warehouse of books to sell and in 1996 founded Ken Sanders
Rare Books. The white brick building is adorned with two
stained-glass windows near the front door. One is of a stego-
saurus, Sanders's favorite dinosaur; the other, pulled from a

demolished Catholic church, is of Saint Jude, the patron saint of lost causes. Inside, the store is so full that if a fourteen-year-old should ever wander in with a list of books in his back pocket, as Sanders had at Bertrand Smith's Acres of Books, he would have enough to keep him enchanted for as long as he wished. On the other hand, if he were to consider slipping out without paying for a book, he would regret it. Sanders has chased these guys down streets and alleys and parking lots. He has taken them to court. He has scared them half to death. He will do whatever possible to get his books back and prevent thieves from ever, ever thinking of stealing another book.

# ❖ 6 ❖

# Happy New Year

It was the start of a new millennium, and Gilkey had nothing but good feelings about the year to come. He had a dream and a thick stack of credit card numbers to make it come true. With the holidays over, his job at Saks was done, and to start the year off right, he decided to take his father to Los Angeles, one of their favorite cities. "We loved the malls, the shops, the weather. There were celebrities there, more opportunities," he said.

One such opportunity arose on a sunny afternoon. Gilkey and his father had lunch at a fancy hotel in Beverly Hills, after which he decided to walk around and check out some of the shops nearby. The neighborhood was wealthy, the kind where

shoppers with drivers were not uncommon, and he was en-
ticed by a small but particularly impressive store with a large
locked area. They were selling rifles for $500,000, jewelry
well into six digits—and books, displayed in neat, becoming
stacks. Gilkey thought he might pick up something small,
with a price tag of about $2,000. (When I asked him what his
father was doing while he was scouting loot, Gilkey said he
was sitting outside, waiting. I doubted this, but became more
interested in why Gilkey was protecting him than I was about
the extent of his father's involvement.) Given the cost of
most items in the store, he thought, surely they wouldn't care
about such a small loss. He looked at the books and took
mental notes about what he wanted. The next day, while
doing his laundry at a laundromat, he called the store from a
pay phone. It was time to use the first of the credit card numbers he had pilfered from Saks.

"I was in your store the other day," said Gilkey. "Do you
still have that first edition of Beatrix Potter's *The Tale of
Mrs. Tittlemouse?*"

The woman put the phone down to check. "Yes," she said,
"we do."

"Well, let me see," said Gilkey, as though he needed to
think about it. "I'll take it." He explained that it was a gift and
asked the woman to wrap it, adding, "Do you mind if I pay
for it now?"

Gilkey gave her the credit card number and finished his laundry. From the laundromat, he called to confirm that the charge had gone through.

"It's ready to go," she said.

"Do you mind if someone else picks it up, because I'm rather busy," said Gilkey. "I'm getting ready for this party." He figured that way when he arrived at the store he wouldn't be expected to be carrying the credit card.

Gilkey raced to the store right before closing time at six. He went in, took a quick glance at the books, and said, "Wow, this is a great place you've got here. He certainly did a great job picking it out." She handed him the book, and he left.

As Gilkey would say, it was that easy.

By now, Sanders's e-mail system had been up and running for several months, and he received notices of theft occasionally, but most of his time was spent attending to his store. While his daughter, Melissa, worked with customers, cataloged new items, stocked shelves, and answered the phone, Sanders attended estate sales, provided appraisals, and also helped customers. Often, he was upstairs at his cluttered desk, writing bibliographic entries. Sanders sells to other shops, collectors, libraries, and other institutions, so when he acquires items that might be of interest, he sends them a bibliographic description. It's a way of drumming up the next month's business. A surprising number of people wander in off the street with boxes or bags full of books they'd like to sell, and Sanders will take a look. Most times, they are not worth much, but occasionally he comes across a gem, like the time a man in his twenties walked into the store with a book his parents had given to him. It was his grandmother's, and they had no idea whether or not it was valuable.

"Uh, I don't want to get your hopes up," Sanders told him, holding the small book, about four by six inches, in the palm of his hand, "but if this is real, it's worth six figures." He told the young man he would need to authenticate it.

It was real: a Mormon *Book of Commandments* from 1833, a precursor to the *Doctrine and Covenants*, one of the three scriptural works of the Mormon Church. At the time, the Mormons were at odds with their neighbors, and in retaliation for Joseph Smith's destruction of an anti-Mormon newspaper, an angry mob stormed the printing press while the book was being printed and threw the printed sheets out the window. The story, which most agree is apocryphal, is that two little Mormon girls gathered up the sheets into their long skirts and hid in the cornfields until the mob had dispersed. From those loose pages, the books were then sewn by hand. Because of their volatile origins, most copies were incomplete, although a title page was added a few years later. Technically, because the books were never finished or professionally bound, the book wasn't ever published. In the past 170 years, only twenty-nine copies have surfaced.[1]

Sanders kept the *Book of Commandments* in a safe-deposit box and later sold it for the young man to a collector for $200,000, from which Sanders earned a commission.[2] Mostly, however, these types of finds don't just show up on dealers' counters. Books go missing far more frequently. But of the theft of *The Tale of Mrs. Tittlemouse*, Sanders had heard nothing. The store owners were not members of the ABAA.

❖❖

THE NEXT MONTHS were busy. In February, armed with a pile of credit card numbers, Gilkey took his father on a two-week trip to France and Germany, where they visited casinos, wineries, restaurants, and museums. They won a moderate but satisfying sum while gambling, which confirmed Gilkey's feelings about his ability to take risks and come out unscathed, at least most of the time. They returned just in time for the Los Angeles Festival of the Book, where Gilkey "picked up" about ten more books, including a signed first-edition *Ragtime*, by E. L. Doctorow. It is number eighty-six on the Modern Library's list of one hundred best English-language novels.

What people choose to collect is revealing. That Gilkey favors books from the Modern Library's list is in keeping with his desire to be admired. He isn't following his own taste as much as that of experts. The books are already sanctioned, surefire greatest hits, guaranteed to impress.

Through the spring, Gilkey kept up his pace, stealing about a book or two a month. He is as adept at justifying these thefts as he was at pulling them off. He explained it to me like this: When he walks into a rare book store and ogles the riches lined up on the shelf, he sees them almost as the personal collection of the store owner. What a wealthy person this is! Look how many books he owns! It is not fair that he charges so much for a single book, Gilkey thinks. Books selling for $10,000 or $40,000 or half a million—they are all out of his reach. How am I to afford it? he asks with righteous indignation. So he takes what he sees as duly his. That dealers pay a lot for their books and, with the exception of relatively few lucky or especially savvy ones, barely make ends meet does not occur to him. Even after I brought this to his attention, he chose not to acknowledge his guilt. As he sees it, if he owns fewer rare books than the next collector or dealer, the world is not fair, and, as he put it, he means to "even the score."

I wondered what fed this skewed perspective of justice. While many collectors build images of themselves through their collections, most of them do not cross the line between coveting and stealing. It was not just a collection Gilkey was building but an image of himself for the world. In this respect, he did not differ from other collectors, but most of them do not cross the line between coveting and stealing. The leap between collector and thief is a huge moral and ethical one. But for Gilkey, who repeatedly crosses the line, having not paid for the books—having acquired them for free, as he would say—adds even more to their allure. He told me that back when he kept his books at his mother's house, before he started secreting them to a storage facility, he separated those he had paid for from those he had stolen, the former on one set of shelves, the latter on another. Stolen or not, however, his satisfaction was always fleeting: the more books a collector gets, the more he wants. In this respect, Gilkey is like any other collector. As collectors have often remarked, collecting is like hunger, and having one more book doesn't quench the longing for another.

As spring headed into summer, Gilkey wanted to get his hands on even more books, but since he was still on parole for stealing foreign currency (to pay for books and living expenses), he felt he should be more circumspect. While he tempered the scope of his acquisitions, he found methods to at least be in proximity to spectacular books. In June, he visited The Huntington Library Museum, in San Marino, California. For lovers of books and art, the place is a paradise; for Gilkey, it must have been mighty fuel for his fantasies.

Henry Huntington, born on February 27, 1850, in Oneonta, New York, grew up in a well-to-do family in a house filled with books.[3] He read and appreciated books throughout his life and, from the age of about twenty-one, acquired them voraciously. Decades later, after founding the Pacific Electric Railway and an intercity transit system in California, he inherited around $30 million and began collecting rare books and manuscripts. In 1919, he founded The Huntington Library, which now has more than seven million rare books, manuscripts, photographs, prints, and maps in the fields of British and American history and literature. The library stacks are open only to scholars, but Gilkey got to see a small selection of items on display for the public.

On view was "The Prologue to the Wife of Bath's Tale" from Geoffrey Chaucer's *The Canterbury Tales*, made in England, c. 1400–1405, an illuminated manuscript on vellum adorned with an intricate border that looks like a fabulously bejeweled vine.[4] Such literary tricking-out seems akin to framing a masterpiece in gold or wrapping an emerald necklace in marbled paper and satin ribbons—an effort to clothe something wondrous in a fitting garment. Another illuminated text on display, a Gutenberg Bible (c. 1455), is similarly bedecked with fantastical borders, and they're still as clear and lovely as freshly stitched silk embroidery. Given the number of times throughout history that books, especially racy or religious texts like these—including the *Kräutterbuch* on my desk, which had illustrations that were at the time of publication considered unfit to be viewed by women[5]—have been snatched up, set into piles in public squares, and set on fire, the fact that these ancient tomes are still around is doubly miraculous.[6] The depth of care and craft in their creation in retrospect seems like an expression of epic optimism. Even though anyone can look up photos of books like these online and view up-close images where every mark on the page is in sharp detail, every year thousands choose to visit the books in person. In addition to being objects of beauty, like all ancient books, they provide a physical link to the past. This is one of their most powerful, enduring effects.

The Huntington's more modern texts are just as alluring. On the title page of the original manuscript of Henry David Thoreau's *Walden*, one can see the author's right-leaning, fluid, elegant script in dark ink. In the lower right corner, smudged ink reminds us that this was written by a real, living, mistake-making human, one whose finger was once stained black from that very point on the page. Gilkey was enchanted by the whole display, but lingered near one volume in particular. He couldn't take his eyes off Samuel Pepys's seventeenth-century diary, noticing how fragile and small it looked sitting in a glass case.

Huntington, like Gilkey, used his collection to influence how people viewed him. A story in the December 25, 1910, issue of the *Los Angeles Examiner* noted that he "delights in having an appreciative book lover call on him, and it is then the railway magnate opens up his cases and brings forth some jewel in his splendid collection and exhibits it to the visitor."

I had heard at least one dealer refer to collecting as a sport, and I got the impression that Huntington was competing to win. A cartoon in the *Los Angeles Times* on March 27, 1920, showed two mustachioed gentlemen in a library and bore the caption: "Henry E. Huntington and Herschel V. Jones, who publishes the Minneapolis Journal and collects rare books, are talking shop out in San Marino." The cartoon summed up the collectors' competitive instincts perfectly. Huntington is saying, "I've just picked up Eve's diary," and Jones replies, "Oh! That reminds me, I got hold of 'The Log of the Ark,' by Noah, the other day!"

❧❧

While still in Los Angeles, on a warm, sunny day, Gilkey drove to the Century Plaza Hotel, one of his favorite spots to conduct business since it had a row of phones with a good deal of privacy. He was also fond of its location: near Melrose Avenue, where there were two bookstores he planned to visit.

From the hotel, Gilkey called one of them, Dailey's Rare Books on Melrose, and asked about a few authors, one of whom was Mark Twain. He was in luck: they had a first edition of *Life on the Mississippi*. He gave them a credit card number and told them someone else would pick up the book, which they said would be fine. Gilkey got there and, to avoid suspicion, took his time. He didn't want to appear rushed or hide behind dark sunglasses, stuttering and stumbling. *Act normal*, he thought. When he left, he ripped up the credit card receipt and threw it in a trashcan, a protective measure he repeated after almost every pickup. He would visit Dailey's two more times in the next year.

Gilkey drove the short distance back to the hotel, speeding because he hates to have anyone cut in front of him in traffic. At the hotel, he called his favorite bookstore, the Heritage Book Shop, also on Melrose. Gilkey has a strong sense of decorum, which comes through on the phone, and a complete lack of guilt about ripping people off, which does not. When he reached the store on the phone, he asked if they had any books by H. G. Wells. They did. He gave them a credit card number and, as usual, said that someone else would stop by to pick it up, a man named Robert. Shortly thereafter, Gilkey went for the pickup.

"Great place you have here," said "Robert." He talked with Ben or Lou (Gilkey wasn't sure) for ten minutes or so and took a look at a few books. The book was already packed up and ready to go, so "Robert" signed for it and walked out with *The Invisible Man*.

❖·❖

GILKEY TOLD ME that when he holds a rare book, he smells its age, feels its crispness, makes sure there's nothing wrong with it, and opens it up very gently. He thumbs through a few pages. If the author is still alive, he thinks about whether he wants it signed. He says that a book like *The Invisible Man* is like a fine wine. It feels good to hold it and, especially, to add it to his collection—but not to read, almost never to read. Like most book collectors, his attachment is not so much to the story as to all that the book represents.

Winston S. Churchill, a bibliophile who paid for his books, nonetheless understood the same intimate attachment:

> "What shall I do with all my books?" was the question;
> and the answer, "Read them," sobered the questioner.

But if you cannot read them, at any rate handle them, and, as it were, fondle them. Peer into them. Let them fall open where they will. Read on from the first sentence that arrests the eye. Then turn to another. Make a voyage of discovery, taking soundings of uncharted seas. Set them back on their shelves with your own hands. Arrange them on your own plan, so that if you do not know what is in them, you at least know where they are. If they cannot be your friends, let them at any rate be your acquaintances. If they cannot enter the circle of your life, do not deny them at least a nod of recognition.[7]

❖❖

BACK IN THE BAY AREA, Gilkey began ordering one book after another. The first one to come to Sanders's attention was a $113 copy of *Toddle Island*, Lord Bottsford's diary from 1894, stolen from Serendipity Books in Berkeley. The owner, Peter Howard, was an old pal of Sanders, someone he often met up with at book fairs around the country. It wasn't an expensive book, but it bothered Sanders just the same.

"Let them steal hubcaps," he would say, "just keep their hands off books."

He sent an e-mail notifying the trade and hoped that *Toddle Island* would be the last theft he heard of for a long time.

Within a couple of months, however, Sanders was getting reports from ABAA members, almost all in Northern California, who appeared to be falling prey to a rash of seemingly random book thefts, the only known connection of which was stolen credit cards. In vitriolic e-mails, Sanders began referring to the perpetrator as the "Northern California Credit Card Thief."

In November 2000, with the holiday season in full swing, Saks hired Gilkey again.

❖ ❖

NORTHERN CALIFORNIA is fertile ground for any book lover, and there is no shortage of collectors. Wandering the aisles of a recent antiquarian book fair in San Francisco, I ran into someone I recognized: an owner of my local pet supplies store, Celia Sack. I was frequently in her store, buying food for my dog and cats, but I had no idea she was a book collector. We said hello, but it wasn't until the next time I visited her store that we began talking books. Sack lights up when the subject arises, and reveals a depth of literary knowledge that reflects her seven years working at a book auction house. I learned that she is an avid collector, as are both her parents, but that none of her friends or family loves books the way she does, so she has no one to share her excitement when she finds a new prize. A few weeks later, she picked up several rare gardening books and cookbooks, and we arranged for me to come over and take a look at them.

Sack lives in a flat within a handsome, modest-sized Victorian house in the Castro district. Her store is filled with 1950s displays and other vintage pet-related objects, and I expected a small group of quirky titles, but that's not what I found. Her dining room had been transformed into an impressive library. The walls, wrapped with built-in shelves, were filled floor to ceiling, mostly with leather- and cloth-bound beauties, and on the heavy wooden table at the room's center lay a couple dozen of her favorites. It was like a private museum, and it made me wonder how many flats in San Francisco harbor secret collections like this. Touring a personal library is a lot like going through someone's family photo album, but in this case one whose photographer was Edward Weston or Roy DeCarava. Like expertly shot photos, each volume had a story behind it, and although she stopped only to pull favorites from the shelves, the tour lasted about an hour and a half.

Sack's areas of interest appeared broad: modern literature and lesbian literature on the left-hand wall, which extended to the next wall and then gave way to Edward Gorey, World War I, natural history, cookbooks, the Pan Pacific Exposition, and how-to books for retailers. Admiring so many lovely and artfully arranged books, I was covetous. I would love to own a library like this—so what was stopping me? Many of the books Sack showed me were not expensive. I buy shoes that cost more. Way more. I suppose that more than anything, I am daunted by the enormity of the endeavor: how much research is necessary to understand what is valuable, along with how much scouting I'd need to do. And once you get into the very valuable books, which I realize not all collectors do, I would have trouble justifying the expense to myself, even though I deem such books worthy and respect others who make the investment. Still, even collectors with little money find ways to buy collectible books. The difference between me and them was that while I desire books, they are compelled to get them. Nothing stops them.

Not all Sack's books were very valuable, monetarily, but all had special meaning to her. Intermingled among inscribed first editions were some that are simply appealing to her. She showed me several of her favorite how-to books, *The Whole Art of Curing, Pickling and Smoking Meat and Fish both in the British and Foreign Modes,* published in 1847, and *Roadside Marketing: A Complete Advisor for the Everyday Use of Gardeners, Fruit Growers, Poultrymen, and Farmers, on the Marketing of their Products to the Consumer Direct,* a Depression-era guide to roadside stands. They were snapshots of history that few people today have ever seen.

Before I left, Sack showed me examples of her favorite type of book, the association copy. Several of them were by lesbian authors, with author-to-lover inscriptions. She held a copy of *No Letters to the Dead,* by Gale Wilhelm, 1936. Inscribing the book to her girlfriend, Helen Hope Rudolph, Wilhelm had written: "Dear Helen—Someone once said this edition looked like a box of chocolates. So—with my love—a box of chocolates worth 6 shillings, Gale."

Looking up, Sack said, "It's like being a witness to an intimate moment in the author's life."

Being a woman and under forty set Sack apart from most book collectors, but I had come across others who didn't fit the mold, either. When I first brought the *Kräutterbuch* to John Windle Books in San Francisco, I noticed a young Hispanic man walking into the store. Windle addressed him by name; he was a regular. It occurred to me how unusual it is to see a person of color at a rare book fair or store. This has been an old-white-man's game for a long time, but it appeared, at that moment, that perhaps things were changing.

Joseph Serrano, thirty-five, grew up in San Francisco with a mother who had read Latin American literature to him when he was a boy. He is a heavyset, amiable man with long-lashed brown eyes behind rectangular wire glasses, who described himself to me thus: "I'm different. I don't have a higher education. I'm not a scholar or anything. I'm just an oddball about books." At the time we met, on his nightstand were Sartre's *No Exit* and Roth's *Portnoy's Complaint* (paperbacks, he assured me, never first editions for reading).

As a child, Serrano's aunt, who had worked as a bookbinder in El Salvador, gave him a set of leather-bound books, and he recognized how special they were. At sixteen, he worked as a delivery boy for a florist in posh Pacific Heights. "Almost every house I went into had a big wall of books," he said. To own such a wall became a dream. At twenty-three, while working as a tow-truck driver, he bought his first valuable book, *Franny and Zooey*, by J. D. Salinger, for $100. "*Catcher in the Rye* is one of my favorites," he said, "but I couldn't afford it." After that first find, he began scouring estate sales, Goodwill and Salvation Army stores. He didn't like driving the tow truck, but the advantage of the job was that between pickups he could study dealers' catalogs, memorize the information, and go on searching expeditions. "I'd walk into a thrift store and I'd know what was valuable," he said. He wanted to make a living out of it, so at first he would spend $2 or $3 for a book and turn it around for $20, $100. He was also assembling his own collection, so he would buy books by obscure authors whose value he recognized, and later trade them for books in the categories he was collecting: Californian, Latin American, and twentieth-century literature. One of his favorite possessions is the first printed description of the Bear Flag Revolt, the 1846 American revolt against the authorities of the Mexican province of California, which later became the state of the same name. "It used to be," said Serrano, "I was happy finding books worth a hundred dollars and paying only a couple bucks for them, but as I learned about books that have changed people, controversial books like Orwell's *1984*, important books—that's what I really want to collect. It's the hunt that keeps it alive. I go to these estate sales where people walk right by the books; they're only interested in furniture or art. Once I sat on the floor and started pulling titles off the shelf: first-edition Hemingways, Faulkners. It was amazing." Like adventurers who still trawl the sea for centuries-old shipwrecks' loot, book hunters' hope and determination is fed by stories like Serrano's. He still visits thrift shops, but he also likes going to fairs and rare book shops, where he can test his knowledge against the dealers'. He has taken what he has learned as an amateur book appraiser and is now building his own rare book business online. He explains the draw like this: "You see something you can't afford, but you buy it anyway," he said. "My wife calls it an addiction, but finding those books is such a good feeling."

Sometimes that good feeling is experienced also by those who help collectors with their searching. Several times, Sanders had mentioned a London man, David Hosein, who travels the world for business and, while doing so, stops by shops for books written by vagabonds and other outsiders. In an e-mail to me, Hosein described his collection:

> My collection is focused on people (iconoclasts, cults and groups) and activities (legal and illegal) outside norms of society. For instance: prison, outlaw bikers, hobos, pimps, druggies, con men, environmental activism, training shoe (sneaker) collectors, pre hip hop culture and Japanese protest books. At the heart of the collection is a large number of works by prisoners.
>
> I have been buying avidly both 20th century first-hand account nonfiction titles and photographic monographs in these areas for more than 10 years. I am only interested in books in fine condition. In this regard I am as nerdy as your regular Stephen King freaks.

Sanders is enamored of this collection's originality—and so am I. In truth, such collections keep the business fresh for collectors and dealers like Sanders, who now keeps an eye out for books by hoboes, vagabonds, and the like, to put aside for him.

"Someone like Hosein," said Sanders, "he's ahead of the curve, pioneering a new collection, and people pay attention to it."

According to Sanders, finding a buyer for a collection as original as Hosein's requires as much ingenuity as building it, and it's more likely that a visionary dealer or institution would purchase it than an individual collector. "After all," Sanders said, "from a collecting point of view, the finding and the acquiring are what fuel the collector and the collection. Often, collectors burn out or let go of collections when they have been so narrowly defined as to preclude the acquisition of any new material. The collection reaches a level of stasis and the collector becomes burned out." A collector like Hosein probably doesn't spend a lot of time worrying about who will buy his books. Amassing a collection like this seems to be a personal quest. But when he decides to sell it, like any collection, the effort put into bringing the books together will pay off; its value will be greater than the sum of its parts.

Even when a book is not part of a collection, if it carries the cachet of being a "classic," its value climbs. A friend gave me an article she came across in *Worth* magazine that said that literary classics have outpaced the stock and bond markets in the past twenty years. A graph boasted an almost cartoon-like upward-reaching line demonstrating what a good investment such a collection can be. Naively, I assumed that this was good news for dealers: if people learned that collecting rare books was a smart investment, business would increase. I wrote to Sanders about it, and he responded in character:

I actually don't think that this is necessarily a good thing. Books should always be acquired for the sheer love and joy of it. Thinking of them as investment objects first turns them into mere widgets and commodities. It reduces their cultural heritage and diminishes not only the books, but their authors and readers as well. Let's leave the pork belly future to Wall Street.

Without Wall Street many forms of books, incunables, high spots of modern literature, are already unobtainable by the average collector or even fairly well-to-do collectors. Think Great Gatsby at over a $100k. . . . Look what happened in the art market, where paintings that used to cost thousands are now hundreds of thousands, and paintings that used to cost hundreds of thousands of dollars are now millions of dollars. . . .

If Wall Street gets hold of books and turns them into high priced investment widgets, then look out. No one will be able to afford them any more and some of the joy of collecting will be gone. The vast bulk of collecting is done in the few hundred to few thousand dollar range. . . .

> If you collect what you love and enjoy, and always buy
> the best you can afford, and buy copies in the best
> condition available, your books will always prove to be a
> good investment.

❖ ❖

IT WASN'T LONG before Gilkey began snagging more receipts at Saks. He regarded it as a business, and his goal was
to pocket two or three credit card numbers a day. His plans
worked without a hitch. *It was fun,* he thought. When he did
pickups, there was a moment of exhilaration, but then it was
time to move on to the next one.

Sometimes Gilkey's help was needed off the floor. He
would call customers to inform them of special events in a
room equipped with a phone, a computer, and a brown envelope filled with receipts. It was a temptation too strong to
resist.

Gilkey wasn't very busy, so he used the computer to research books and peruse booksellers' websites. Once he had
decided on something he would like, always an author or
title he had heard of, he would wait for his lunch break, then
head to a nearby hotel, one like the Crowne Plaza or the
St. Francis, any that had phones with privacy. He never called

in a book order from Saks, for fear the call would be traced to him.

After a while, though, his success seemed too good to be true. He became suspicious of exceedingly wealthy customers. Gilkey said that when the CEO of Netscape bought shoes, he resisted the urge to pocket the receipt. Once, when the chairman called about a shoe, and Gilkey's manager asked him to go to the shoe department to help out, he thought it was a trap. That day, one platinum card–wielding customer after another approached him, buying $800 shoes, $900 shoes. He felt sure that Saks was onto him, putting temptation in his way. At the end of the day, he ripped up all the receipts he had pocketed.

His fears about Saks were unfounded. But in January 2001, when Gilkey's parole officer learned that he was working in San Francisco, he put a stop to it. The terms of his parole had included staying in Modesto, so the officer told Gilkey to find a job there instead. Gilkey was incensed. Working at Saks had been one of the best things that had happened to him. It was easy work, he got to dress nicely, and he liked his coworkers. Most important, of course, the job offered him proximity to all those high-limit credit cards. Plus, he had just started working another part-time job in San Francisco, conducting audience surveys for a movie distributor, which was almost as good a gig as the job at Saks.

He was working in the movie industry, he told himself, and for someone with a fascination with celebrity, it was exciting. But when that employer did a background check on Gilkey and found he had a criminal record, he was fired. He had been working there only two weeks.

As if being forced out of his jobs was not bad enough, on January 14, the Oakland Raiders, Gilkey's favorite football team, lost an AFC championship game to the Baltimore Ravens, and they lost big: 16 to 3. He and his father had watched the game together, and they were sure the Raiders would be victorious. When they weren't, Gilkey felt as slighted as he had by the parole officer. So he did what he usually did when he felt wronged: he stole a book, this time using a bad check. It was momentary succor for perceived injustices. He figured it was harmless, only $200, but the police were notified, and he was arrested.

According to Gilkey, in court, the public defender suggested they claim mental defect, which Gilkey considered a terrific idea. But when the judge told him he would spend a year in a mental institution, Gilkey told him, "Forget that. There's nothing wrong with me," and agreed to a sentence of six and a half months. The way sentences for this type of offense go, he knew that the actual time spent behind bars would likely be half that time. Gilkey then requested a delay, and the judge agreed to set his starting date in June, four months away. Fired up by the loss of his jobs and a prison sentence he considered unfair, Gilkey knew exactly how he would spend his time.

*You want to fight?* he thought. His challenge was directed at the world, with particular aim at rare book dealers. *Then it's war.*

## ✦ 7 ✦

# Trilogy of Kens

With four months until Gilkey was to begin his sentence, he and his father drove up and down the coast of California, staying for days at a time in Lake Tahoe, San Francisco, Los Angeles, San Diego, sometimes making stops at the family's home in Modesto. It was an extended vacation with an impending end, paid for with Gilkey's father's savings and stolen credit card numbers.

On March 14, they stayed at a hotel at the San Francisco airport, because parking was cheaper than at hotels downtown. It was a lovely day, and they set out in a rental car to the Westin Hotel. There, Gilkey opened the Yellow Pages and turned to the listings for rare book stores. He had already done preliminary research on his computer in Modesto and was especially impressed by the extensive collection of the Brick Row Book Shop. As he dialed their number, he pulled a credit card receipt from his pocket.

Gilkey identified himself as Dan Weaver and spoke with Andrew Clark, who was impressed with "Weaver" and treated him with respect because he seemed to be just the sort of person who might become a good customer.

"I'm looking for a gift," said "Weaver," in his polite voice. "Something in the two-thousand-to-three-thousand-dollar range. Maybe Thackeray's *Vanity Fair*."

"I'm afraid we haven't got it," said Clark. "But I've got another nineteenth-century novel you might be interested in: *The Mayor of Casterbridge*, by Thomas Hardy."

"Hmm . . ." "Weaver" seemed to be considering.

"It's a two-volume set," added Clark, "with brown half morocco by Riviere, marbled sides, gilt decorated and lettered spines. A first edition, fine copy, twenty-five hundred."

"Well, I think that fits the bill," said "Weaver," who then read his credit card number to Clark and said he would pick up the book later that afternoon.

Clark carefully wrapped *The Mayor of Casterbridge* in plain brown paper and, before heading out to lunch, informed owner John Crichton that someone was going to stop by and pick it up.

Later that day, a man in his late seventies rushed into the store. He told Crichton he was there to pick up a book for his son, Dan Weaver.

"I'm in a hurry"—he scowled—"double-parked. I gotta get the book."

Crichton checked to make sure the credit card charge had been authorized. It had, so he handed over the book with a copy of the invoice.

Gilkey's father rode the elevator down, climbed into the rental car, and gave the book to him.

Gilkey would later explain to me that the reason his father picked up the book was that he needed to use a bathroom, so Gilkey sent him in to take care of his needs and do the pickup. He insisted that his father did not know that he (Gilkey) had purchased the book with a stolen credit card number. But his father had said he was there to pick up a book for Dan Weaver; there was no way he was unaware of his complicity. Again, Gilkey's fierce denial of his father's role was more perplexing than his father's involvement, although both continued to bewilder me.

To Gilkey, having a book like *The Mayor of Casterbridge*—old and fine, a piece of literary history—in his hands, felt deeply satisfying. There was nothing like it. He held it, knowing that it was worth something, that "everyone wanted it," but that he was the only one who owned it. It was thrilling. When he was done examining it, he carefully laid it down in the backseat. He was a little nervous during the pickup, but his father had come through fine. They were both relieved as they drove away.

A month later, the real Dan Weaver, legitimate owner of the credit card, called Crichton and demanded, "Why did you charge me twenty-five hundred dollars—and for a *book*?!" Crichton looked into it and discovered that the order was indeed fraudulent. How could this have happened? He had once been security chair of the ABAA, and he was careful. At once, he e-mailed Sanders and gave him the details. Sanders immediately sent an e-mail to the ABAA and ILAB, noting the content of the thief's phone calls to Brick Row, the physical particulars of the stolen copy of *The Mayor of Caster-bridge*, and most important, a description of the thief: elderly, pretty shabby-looking, gruff voice.

Now everyone could be on the lookout.

A couple of months later, Gilkey was eager to get a book from another county. He had been having one success after another and was feeling bold, confident. He called Heldfond Book Gallery in San Anselmo, a small town in Marin County, just north of San Francisco. He spoke with proprietor Lane Heldfond, telling her he was on the road and wanted to buy a couple of gifts: a children's book and an autographed book. Heldfond suggested *The Patchwork Girl of Oz*, listed at $1,800, and *Joseph in Egypt*, a book by one of Gilkey's favorite authors, Thomas Mann, autographed and priced at

$850. He said that he was, at that moment, looking at their website, which was a careless slip, since he had just said he was calling from the road,[1] but Heldfond, who noticed the slip, didn't call him on it. Gilkey told her his cousin would pick up the books the next day.

The next day was sunny and clear, so Gilkey decided to take a ferry across the Bay. San Anselmo is a sleepy little town, one of the few in wealthy Marin County that still benefits from the charm of disheveled thrift stores and coffee shops that pour coffee-to-go into cups without logos. Occupying the angled end of a wedge-shaped building, Heldfond Gallery is a triangular shop with a small cushioned window seat at its tightest corner. Heldfond is a petite woman in her forties, with olive skin, long, wavy dark hair, and a disarming smile. In addition to working as a bookseller, she is a sculptor, and her visual sense is reflected on the shelves. Heldfond and her husband, Erik, had both been lifelong collectors when they opened the store in 1991. They bought what they could afford and hoped prices would rise; they were usually right, because despite the tough climate for mom-and-pop stores, the business grew.

After Gilkey placed his order for the two books, Heldfond hung up and called to her husband.

"Something's not right," she said. She had a bad feeling about the order. It had been too easy.

"Was the charge authorized?" he asked.

It was, so he assured her there was nothing to worry about.

Heldfond pulled the books from the shelves—*Joseph in Egypt* in its somber black covers, *The Patchwork Girl of Oz* in its vibrantly illustrated dust jacket—wrapped them in paper, and set them under the counter.

When Gilkey arrived in San Anselmo, he walked to the post office a block away from the store and placed another call to Heldfond to make sure the order had gone through. It had.

At the threshold of Heldfond Book Gallery, Gilkey looked around to make sure there weren't any undercover cops' cars parked on the street, then walked in with one hand covering his mouth.

"I've just come from the dentist," he said to Heldfond, talking out of the side of his mouth in an effort to distort his voice so that she would not recognize it as the caller's. He knew it was a gamble and began to feel agitated. After all, he was supposed to be the caller's cousin. He decided to skip the small talk; he stayed in the doorway and left as soon as he got the books, making a run for the bus stop once he was out of view. Now he had two more books to deliver to the storage facility.

On a wall in Heldfond Gallery hung a bookmark with a

quotation from Oscar Wilde: "I can resist everything except temptation."

✦ ✦

I BEGAN to sense that the urge to collect is not born all of a sudden, but gains momentum after, say, one or two purchases. I wondered, if I bought a few first editions of books that had inspired me in my own writing, whether I might feel what collectors felt: I might actually become one of them. A good place to start would be first editions of some of my favorite works of narrative nonfiction: *In Cold Blood*, *The Spirit Catches You and You Fall Down*, *The Professor and The Madman*, *The Orchid Thief*. I began perusing online booksellers' websites to get a sense for how much they would cost. As I read descriptions of inscriptions and other one-of-a-kind traits, I felt the first stirrings of what I imagined was the collector's hunger.

In reading about this hunger, I had repeatedly come across evidence of the widespread fondness for first editions. Other than original manuscripts, they are the closest most readers can get to an author. This sense of a book as an extension of a person is not remotely new. In 1644, John Milton wrote: "For books are not absolutely dead things, but do contain a potency of life in them to be as active as that soul whose progeny they are; nay they do preserve as in a vial the purest efficacy and extraction of that living intellect that bred them."[2] Nearly three hundred years later, in 1900, Walt Whitman echoed that sentiment: "Camerado! this is no book, / Who touches this touches a man."[3] A collector of paintings can get his hands on the one and only; a book collector's best option, aside from the original manuscript, is the first edition. Collectors can't get enough of them. But according to a riddle I came across, this predilection can be problematic: Which man is happier, "he that hath a library with well nigh unto all the world's classics, or he that hath thirteen daughters? The happier man is the one with thirteen daughters, because he knoweth that he hath enough."[4]

I plunged forward anyway and decided to start with a couple of books by Gay Talese, since he would soon be coming through San Francisco and might sign them. I had been warned about the dangers of ordering books from non-ABAA dealers, but I was in a hurry, and the few ABAA dealers I called didn't have what I was looking for. I ordered first editions of *The Overreachers* and *The Bridge*, about $40 each, from two non-ABAA dealers I found online. When they arrived, I eagerly opened the bubble-wrapped packages. *The Overreachers* was in "very good" shape, my first first edition! *The Bridge*, while also in "very good" shape, was not a first edition at all—where *The Overreachers'* copyright page clearly identified it as a "First Edition," *The Bridge* made no mention of its printing. I had no idea what edition it was. I contacted the dealer, who admitted that she was mistaken and agreed to reimburse me the difference in price. Lesson learned.

Gay Talese did sign my copy of *The Overreachers*, and when I brought it home, I put it on the shelf with my non–first editions. I felt that maybe it needed a place of greater honor, but I never got around to moving it. Having touched the pages of a Flaubert manuscript at the New York book fair, I could appreciate why someone might want an original manuscript. Yet, I had to admit, I could not fully grasp the ardor for printed first editions. So much of collecting is driven by emotions, probably most of it, and although I understood the attraction of first editions intellectually, I didn't *feel* it. The strongest attachments I have to books are those with which I have a personal history. When I was a child sick with the flu, my mother gave me her childhood copy of *Anne of Green Gables*. I was as charmed by its old-fashioned beauty as I was by the story. It had faded taupe linen with an illustration of Anne in profile on the cover. Inside was an inscription: "To Florence from Aunt Freddie, Xmas 1911," meaning that not only had my mother read it, but also her mother, Florence. I also treasure my father's vividly illustrated *Peter Rabbit* (in which Peter looks like a lunatic with devilish eyes) and his family of cat books (*Mother Cat, Fluffy*

*Kitty, Muffy Kitty*, and, best of all, *Puffy Kitty*). Of all my grandparents' books, none is more bewitching than *Lettres de mon moulin*, a 1948 book with lovely watercolor illustrations of French country life. (Does the fact that I adore a book I cannot read a single word of indicate at least some leaning toward bibliomania?) It has a soft cover with an illustration of a windmill and is wrapped in cracked glassine. The way it obscures the illustration makes me think of an old train's window. None of these books is of any value in the marketplace (I checked), but I will always appreciate them for the stories they hold, both on the page (those in English, that is) and in their histories. I doubt I'd feel any different if they were first editions—unless they were worth enough, say, to pay for my children's education, in which case I'd have to part with them. But it would be a sad parting.

So my Talese first edition sat on my shelf wedged between my second or third or twelfth editions of other books. As passionate as I am about reading, and as appreciative as I am of the aesthetic, historic charms of old books, the collecting bug hadn't caught me yet.

❖ ❖

When Lane Heldfond was notified that the credit card number used for the purchase of the first editions of *Joseph in Egypt* and *The Patchwork Girl of Oz* was fraudulent, she was shocked, but assumed insurance would cover their loss— enough money, she realized, for her and Erik and their six-year-old daughter to take a vacation in Hawaii. She was mistaken; insurance didn't cover it. (Unless merchants obtain signatures from bona fide cardholders, they must absorb the cost of the stolen goods.) Furious, she e-mailed Ken Sanders the details. She had read his recent notices, and unlike so many of her colleagues who are loath to expose their vulnerability, she felt it was important to get word out of their missing books. She wrote that a fairly knowledgeable man had called about buying books as gifts. Like the thief Sanders had warned the trade about, he had used a credit card to pay for them and said a relative would pick them up. But this thief was not elderly. He was in his thirties, she guessed, with dark hair.

Sanders had been sending "Northern California Credit Card Thief" notices to the trade, but maybe he was wrong. Maybe it was "thieves" he should be warning them about. Was this a gang? He felt as though he were chasing phantoms. His detective work might have been easier had all his fellow dealers been willing to talk about their losses.

❖❖

THE PLEASURE of Gilkey's extended vacation with his father was heightened by his success at getting so much for free. Gilkey had two ways to wrangle a night in a hotel: using a stolen credit card number or telling hotel management that the toilet in his room had overflowed, thereby getting a refund. He found that most hotels guaranteed one-hundred-percent satisfaction, so if he complained to the general manager, most of the time they wouldn't charge him. The same went for meals. Only a couple of times did his methods not work: at the St. Francis Hotel, in San Francisco, where they held his luggage until he could come up with cash to cover the room, and at the Mandarin Oriental, also in San Francisco, where he'd stayed because he had wanted to experience a five-star hotel. When they didn't offer a refund after he said the toilet overflowed, he cleared the room of the shampoos, soaps, and complimentary slippers, which gave him a small sense of vindication.

As the weeks passed, and June drew near, Gilkey picked up his pace, about two books a week. Although it wasn't very valuable, one of his favorites was Stephen King's *The Dead Zone*, because of how he got it. One of the greatest pleasures of beholding one's collection is remembering how each volume came to rest on the shelf. Gilkey had ordered *The Dead Zone* from a pay phone in the Beverly Hills library, right across the street from the police station.

This was an exciting time for Gilkey. He took precautions, always watching book dealers closely to see if something was wrong in case they'd called the police. He made up rules for himself: appear relaxed, chat for five to ten minutes, always check for suspicious cars or people, make sure the bookseller doesn't seem nervous, compliment the stock. While he usually picked up the books himself, sometimes he would use a taxicab driver. He would tell the driver, "I'm lazy, I'll give you a good tip." Or to give the impression that he was not up to the task himself, he would limp, or say he had a headache, or that he wasn't feeling well. He figured cabbies were "greedy enough, they would do anything for money, even five dollars." Once, he considered wearing the costume of a priest during a pickup, but felt he had to draw the line somewhere.

Between January and June of 2001, Gilkey was picking up books worth $2,000, $5,000, $10,000. Together, they totaled at least $100,000. He realized that at this rate if he were to stop working entirely and dedicate himself to book collecting, he might end up with a collection worth millions.

He sensed, however, that he might be setting a pattern that would attract attention, especially in Northern California. So he decided he would expand his reach, steal from one major rare book store after another, and get himself fifty rare books. If the authorities were looking for a pattern, they wouldn't find one. He would order one book from Oregon, another from Idaho, and yet another from Arizona. He'd hit New York, Philadelphia, all over the world. He knew that the market was international, so, as he said, "I could buy a rare book in Argentina, another in England, in South Africa, the Bahamas."

He also decided to change his MO and stop picking up the books himself (or having someone else do it). Instead, he would have them delivered to hotels, where he would pick them up later. It wasn't necessary to tell the bookseller it was a hotel; he could just give them an address.

In June, Gilkey finally went to jail to serve time for the bad check he'd written back in January. He would have three and a half months behind bars to think about his next moves. Before he left, he told his father to disregard his past vow.

"Forget about an estate," he said, "I'm going to build us an empire."

✦✦

AFTER SERVING his sentence, Gilkey walked out the doors of Los Angeles County Jail and within several weeks was hired again at Saks Fifth Avenue. Over the next year, while on parole, he sold expensive designer garments, surreptitiously jotted down the credit card numbers of customers who bought them, then used the numbers to steal, according to his estimate, about a book a month, maybe more.

By the end of 2002, with the holiday shopping season in

full swing, Gilkey's employers were so pleased with his performance they offered him a promotion to the customer service center, where he would have access to cash, plus all the credit slips and gift cards. Fearing the move might trigger a background check that would reveal his criminal history, he tried to decline the offer. His caution was inconsistent, though. When his boss persisted and pushed some forms on him, Gilkey carelessly wrote down his Modesto address, where in 1998 he had done sixty days in jail for writing a bad check. Arriving at work one morning shortly after that, he was summoned by the VP of human resources, who confronted him with his falsified records, and that was the end of his employment.

Gilkey had enjoyed his job at Saks more than any other. His coworkers were nice to him, and customers seemed to appreciate his cordiality, all of which a coworker from the men's department, Tony Garcia, confirmed. "Mostly quiet, very professional" is how Garcia described Gilkey. "Always willing to help."[5]

Being forced to leave made Gilkey feel once again that the world had been unfair to him, singled him out. With his stockpile of receipts, though, he had the means to get even. Just thinking about it brightened his mood.

A couple of weeks later, on Tuesday, January 28, 2003, Gilkey woke at his mother's house and got dressed. He skipped breakfast, took the bus to downtown Modesto, wandered around a little, then went to the Doubletree Hotel, where he settled into a comfortable chair next to the phones in a spacious alcove off the lobby. Gilkey was scrupulous about keeping records, of both books he desired and books he stole, noting which credit cards he had used and the circumstances of each swindle. One of his rules was not to place more than two or three orders in one day, but since not all his attempts would necessarily be fruitful, that morning's list included seven or eight places to call. In addition to books, Gilkey had his heart set on a few antique documents and an antique sterling silver baby rattle he had seen in a catalog. He reached a dealer in Idaho and successfully ordered a copy of *The Monkey Wrench Gang*, coincidentally by Sanders's friend Edward Abbey. Gilkey had the book shipped to an address in Palo Alto that was actually the Westin Hotel.

Gilkey then called a dealer in New York, and another in Chicago, but either they didn't have what he was looking for or the credit card numbers were rejected. Last, he dialed the number of Ken Lopez, a dealer in western Massachusetts. He had noticed Lopez's advertisement in *Firsts*, the magazine devoted to book collecting. He identified himself as Heath Hawkins[6] and said he wanted to get something in the $5,000 to $7,000 range. "Hawkins" then asked about their copy of *The Grapes of Wrath*, by John Steinbeck. Lopez described the book for him, noting that it cost $6,500, and the two men chatted for a while. "Hawkins" seemed genial and somewhat knowledgeable. After their discussion, Lopez agreed to bring the price down to $5,850.

Then "Hawkins" asked Lopez if he thought he should have a clamshell box made for the book, and something clicked in Lopez's memory. About six months earlier, another man, "Andrew Meade," had called him, inquiring about a first edition of *One Flew Over the Cuckoo's Nest*, by Ken Kesey, priced at $7,500—and he had asked about having a clamshell box made. The credit card had not gone through, and although "Meade" had said he would call back with another credit card number, he never did, because it was Gilkey, and he had only one card in Meade's name.

Lopez knew that a colleague of his, Kevin Johnson of Royal Books in Baltimore, had also been hit by "Andrew Meade" months before and lost a first edition of Jack Kerouac's *On the Road*, worth $4,500. Lopez had read enough of Sanders's e-mail warnings about the "Nor Cal Credit Card Thief" to be fairly certain that he had the man they were looking for on the line. After "Hawkins" gave Lopez an American Express number, Lopez told him he'd run the order through, and that "Hawkins" should call him back. A quick call to American Express revealed that the address "Hawkins" had given him was not the one listed on the account.

When "Hawkins" called back, Lopez asked him, "What about this billing address?"

"Oh, yeah," said "Hawkins," "that's not the billing address. The billing address is actually in New York."

"Oh, really?" said Lopez.

"Hawkins" then gave the correct billing address.

"I'm going to run this order through again," said Lopez. "So why don't you call back in a few minutes."

Lopez quickly Googled the shipping address "Hawkins" had given him. It was the Sheraton Hotel in Palo Alto, just down the street from the Westin. (Gilkey was planning to pick up both books on the same day.) Lopez called American Express, who contacted the cardholder, Heather Hawkins, in New York, and asked if she had ordered a rare book. She had no idea what they were talking about.

When "Hawkins" called back to make sure the order had gone through, Lopez's partner asked him to hold a moment while Lopez completed a call on another line. The man on the other line was Ken Sanders, whom Lopez had just alerted to what was going on. When Sanders heard the details, he suggested that Lopez string "Hawkins" along, complete the order, and agree to send the book by overnight delivery. After hanging up, Lopez picked up the other line, where "Hawkins" was waiting, and confirmed that the order was ready to go.

While Gilkey was pleased that he'd "nailed it," Sanders

wasted no time. He contacted San Jose police detective Ken Munson, whom Kevin Johnson, the Baltimore dealer, had spoken with when he filed a complaint about *On the Road* having been stolen. Sanders reminded Munson of that theft and the string of other thefts he suspected were committed by this man "Hawkins" with whom Lopez had just spoken. The "trilogy of Kens," as Sanders calls himself, Lopez, and Munson, got to work.

Detective Munson is a reader of detective novels, Michael Connelly's especially.[7] He's an inquisitive man, often bored by the usual Internet fraud cases he pursues, and was intrigued by this guy stealing books. It wasn't the kind of case he usually took on, especially since the victim was a citizen of Massachusetts, not San Jose; but his high-tech unit, which dealt mostly with fraud, was fairly autonomous. And it was true that the hotel was in his jurisdiction.

Once Munson got Sanders's message, he had to work fast: the book—a facsimile library edition Lopez had sent, in case the sting was not successful—was to be delivered the next morning. Munson thought this thief seemed pretty sharp. The dealers and credit card holders he had ripped off wouldn't know of the fraud until a month or two afterward, when the bills arrived. And once notified, when they looked back over their records, all the dealers would find was a phone number, which would turn out to be a pay phone, and an address, which would turn out to be a hotel. Plus, this thief had been hitting different geographic areas, different jurisdictions. Even if the police could get a warrant on some-body in another state, the DA was not going to spend a thou-sand dollars to have him extradited, or pay his airfare. Munson had come across criminals who know that if they steal a small enough amount from a large enough group of people from different states, they may never be touched. He figured Gilkey was one of them. Munson agreed with Sand-ers and Lopez that whoever had stolen from Kevin Johnson was probably the same thief who had just called Lopez. Worst case, he thought, they'd spend five hours on it, and call it off if the thief didn't show.

Munson contacted the Sheraton and found that there was a reservation for Heather and Heath Hawkins, which Gilkey had made shortly before he asked the hotel to hold all his packages. The hotel sits near Stanford University and ap-pears to suffer from a split personality: Spanish-style archi-tecture (stucco arches, red-tiled roofs) on the outside, pan-Asian details (Chinese lions, lacquered screens) on the inside. Also inside now were two undercover detectives, a woman and a man, seated comfortably in jeans and polo shirts, looking like a couple on vacation. They had arrived early, to be sure to be there for the FedEx delivery, which was guaranteed by ten thirty. They assumed the thief would try to arrive soon after the delivery. Outside, Munson had set up surveillance with unmarked cars in the parking lot. Inside, hotel employees had been alerted to give a signal when "Hawkins" came up to the desk and asked for his package. Of course, none of them really had any idea who or what they were looking for. The thief could be a man, a woman, two men—they didn't know.

While Munson waited, Sanders tried to organize his colleagues. In order to convict Gilkey, he e-mailed them, they needed to send any information about recent thefts that matched Gilkey's MO as soon as possible.

The responses poured in, but not all were helpful.[8] A dealer from New York wrote that she had been approached twice by a man who said that he was buying books for the child of his girlfriend, but because she had found that the shipping addresses had not matched the billing addresses, she had not put the orders through.

Sanders wrote back: *I need details. If he approaches you again, please play along and agree to send the book. Right this minute a motel in California is being staked out by police and he's expecting The Grapes of Wrath in the morning. If all goes well, he'll be in jail this time tomorrow. Confidential . . . if we don't get him, we need to run another sting operation.*

Later that day, Peter Howard, of Serendipity Books in

Berkeley, wrote to Sanders about having lost two books in 2000 to a man who had sent his elderly "uncle" in to pick them up.

Then Erik Heldfond of Heldfond Book Gallery, where Gilkey had stolen two books in 2001, wrote to Sanders that his wife, Lane, had been in the store that day. At the time, she believed she was handing the books to the caller's cousin. *It might be helpful for her to see a photo of guy in custody, as she has a sharp eye and longgggg memory,* he wrote. She estimated that he was *in his late 20s, early 30s, 5'9", brown hair, medium build, clean shaven, GAP type attire.* She noted that he didn't speak normally, saying he'd just come from the dentist.

Ed Smith, of Washington, reminded Sanders that he had lost a *Catch-22* by Joseph Heller, *near fine in dust jacket, real clean copy and a 1/99 ltd. ed. book by Samuel Beckett titled No Knife bound in leather and with a glassine wrapper in a box (fine condition, as new).* Of the sting, he wrote: *Great news . . . mums still the word, right?*

Shortly after, Sanders sent an e-mail to the trade, summarizing what they had learned so far and asking dealers who had been victims if they thought they might be able to identify the thief in a photo lineup.

Gilkey spent the night in the Windham Hotel in San Francisco. The next morning, he emptied his pockets of anything that might identify him, taking only his hotel room key, a phone card, a couple of credit card receipts, and $20 to use for lunch. At around eleven A.M., he boarded the Caltrain for the hourlong ride. Out the window he watched graffiti-smothered industrial buildings speed by, then the back sides of down-and-out neighborhoods, and eventually the palm trees and foreign-car dealerships on the edge of Palo Alto. There, he got off the train and walked two short blocks to the Sheraton.

Strolling through the parking lot, Gilkey noticed the FedEx truck outside. If the book had not yet been delivered, it would be momentarily. As he approached the front desk, he thought he heard a click and people talking, the way they do on a police radio, but decided it was nothing and ignored it. He was just a few feet away from getting *The Grapes of Wrath.*

When Gilkey asked for his package, the hotel clerk went to a back area where they kept the mail. Seconds later, the undercover agents handcuffed him, announcing he was under arrest. They radioed Munson, who was waiting in the parking lot.

"I'm just coming from San Francisco," Gilkey explained, "on my way to the Stanford library to do some research."

"So what are you doing here?" Munson asked him.

"A man on Caltrain offered to pay me twenty bucks to pick up a book for him here."

Munson doubted the story and thought Gilkey looked "nervous and shifty-eyed," but he had dealt with significant cases of fraud in which a transient was paid to do a pickup. There was a chance the story was true.

"Okay, let's take this a step further," said one of the officers. "We're going to unhandcuff you, take you back to the Caltrain station, give you the package—and you go meet the man, point him out to us."

"And don't try to run," one of the officers warned him. "We'll be following you."

Gilkey considered the warning as he walked to the Caltrain station with a half-dozen police officers following him. Stanford University was about a mile away, and if he made a mad dash for it, he might just lose the cops. *What's the worst thing that can happen?* he wondered. *I don't think they will shoot me.* But a mile was a long way. As the undercover officers followed him, he secretly chewed up the credit card receipts in his pocket and spat them out. They reached the station, but instead of running, he stalled for time, approaching various people, asking them if they had seen the man he'd told the police about.

Munson asked the people working at Caltrain if there had been a man hanging around who fit Gilkey's description of him: white male, forty to fifty, white hair, walking with a cane. There had not. After Gilkey had wandered around the station for about thirty minutes, it was pretty clear to the officers that he was lying. They took him in for questioning.

At the police station, Gilkey presented himself as a helpful citizen who had only been trying to assist a man with a cane who couldn't walk very well.[9] While he told the officers his name, he wouldn't answer other questions, such as where he lived. They took the hotel card key in his pocket, but he wouldn't tell them which hotel it was from. Munson then discovered that Gilkey, who had actually given them his real name, was on probation.

And then it began to unravel. Gilkey told the police that the man on the train had instructed him, "Just pick up the book that's waiting for Heath Hawkins," yet at the counter he had said, "I'm picking up the book for Heather Hawkins." Heather Hawkins was the name on the credit card.

"So how did you know the name Heather? You told us just Heath," asked Munson.

"Oh yeah, maybe the guy told me Heather and Heath Hawkins," said Gilkey.

"You're lying," said Munson.

Gilkey, who seemed quite calm at this point, fecklessly stuck with his story, but Munson had a toehold. Then, in Gilkey's pocket, Munson found a crumpled prepaid phone card, which the telephone company traced to three calls made at 10:11, 10:56, and 11:25 A.M. the previous day. They were all to Ken Lopez, the Massachusetts dealer.

"Oh yeah, I was lying to you then," said Gilkey, meaning his slip with the name on the credit card, "but I'm not lying to you now."

He was off to jail.

## ❖ 8 ❖

# Treasure Island

Gilkey was to be held in jail for two days. Sanders e-mailed bookseller Ed Smith, a possible Gilkey victim:

> Subject: Do you know the way to San Jose?
>
> As you know, we got him. But only for 48 hours. We are frantically trying to help the detective with facts to prove a case with the DA on Friday morning.
>
> He's a lying sumbitch (of course). They always are.
>
> I need to hear from more people.

The next day, more reports of thefts flew in.

As suggested, Munson e-mailed Lane Heldfond of Heldfond Book Gallery a series of photos and asked if she could identify the thief. In addition to having a good memory in general, Heldfond's recollection of faces is particularly acute. After looking at the six photos, she said one of them looked very close, but that the man's complexion appeared to be a little ruddier, he had a bit less hair, and his face seemed puffier than the man she remembered. These were subtle differences, but she picked up on them nonetheless.

Munson, impressed by Heldfond's powers of observation, explained to her why the man looked different. Gilkey had been on medication for alopecia, a hair-loss condition, which makes the skin both reddish and a bit bloated. Not only had she identified him correctly, she had identified how his face, which she had seen for only a minute in 2001, had changed.

Heldfond had nailed it. Now Munson had a positive ID.

On February 1, 2003, Sanders e-mailed ABAA members to relay details of the sting and to let them know that Gilkey had met bail (he had used money from a savings account) and been released. "Whereabouts unknown."

Immediately, Sanders's e-mail inbox filled with a flurry of appreciative e-mails. Even if Gilkey had been set free, thanks to Sanders's efforts, the bookselling community was closer than ever to recovering its books and putting the thief behind bars.

❖·❖

ALTHOUGH THEFT has always been a threat to rare book dealers, in the past century, nothing has made it easier for thieves to sell their ill-gotten goods than the Internet. In all my conversations with Ken Sanders, the only subject that riled him as much as news of a recent theft was eBay. It's not only hot property that shows up on that website, but fraud of all sorts, he says. Even sellers with honorable intentions don't necessarily know a first edition from a book club edition—and some don't even know a first edition from a later edition, as I had learned firsthand. Others know perfectly well, but are out to swindle naive buyers.

"A woman here in the valley called me up," said Sanders, "and she says, 'I just purchased an autographed *Catcher in the Rye* on eBay for fifteen hundred.' And I stopped her right there. I said, 'Look, I don't want to see this book, I don't want you to bring it to my store. It's no good, it's a fake. You got taken. Go get your money back.' You cannot buy any kind of real J. D. Salinger–autographed book for ten times that, let alone *The Catcher in the Rye*. I tried to point it out to her. I said, 'Look, why do you think that of the hundreds of sophisticated collectors and booksellers out there, you would be the lucky one?' It's one of the most desired and difficult twentieth-century autographs to get—on the most desired book. Of course it's not the first edition! Because forgers aren't going to ruin a valuable first edition. They're going to pick a worthless edition and put the autograph on that."

One of the reasons people are so ripe for the rip-off, according to Sanders, is what he calls the "*Antiques Roadshow/eBay* syndrome." Due to the television show (where he has since appeared as a rare book expert) and the website, there's much more awareness of books' potential value, but buyers aren't equipped with enough knowledge to guard themselves against fraud.

"People call me up and say, 'I got a first edition of *Gone With the Wind*!'" said Sanders. "Well, no they don't." (To start, there were more than a hundred first editions printed, each labeled as such, but only those from the very first run with "Published May, 1936" are true first editions. Finding one in collectible condition, especially with a jacket, is next to impossible.) "They don't know what a first edition is. But they know it means something good, they know it means something valuable. And that's from watching too many *Antiques Roadshow*s. Mix that with the speed of the Internet and the nine-hundred-pound gorilla that's eBay—any law enforcement person will tell you eBay is the largest legalized fence in the universe."

I called a computer systems security analyst named Mark Seiden for a less impassioned opinion (all of Sanders's opinions are impassioned), but he echoed Sanders almost word for word, saying, "eBay is the largest legalized fence of stolen property in the world." He said that eBay has avoided liability because they are not technically auctioneers, since there is no person hosting, no physical place where the auctions are held. "They say they are a marketplace," said Seiden. "Period." But however legal the business is, the fact is that unscrupulous sellers flourish there.

In another conversation with Sanders, I relayed Seiden's confirmation, which got him fired up again. He told me he sees forgeries on eBay all the time. "I once saw that a guy was selling a John Lennon signature for a dollar," he said. "So I called the buyer and asked if he had got an appraisal. He tells me, 'Those rare book dealers wanted to charge me a hundred dollars for an appraisal.' So I asked him, 'Why not get one? If it's real, you've got a five-thousand-dollar signature.' He told me to eat shit and die."

Sanders told me that several years ago he and his ABAA colleague Ken Lopez met with representatives of eBay, suggesting strategies to combat fraud, to no avail. "Lopez and I, we wasted nine months in negotiations with eBay," said Sanders. "They never followed a single suggestion. They kept stringing us along, but they never changed one single thing."

Ironically, one of the reasons people are getting cheated, according to Sanders, is the practice of providing certificates of authenticity.

"When material comes in," he said, explaining the dealer's traditional process, "you try to establish its provenance, but in many cases it's impossible to do, so the trail ends at some point. You just have to look at the material, the situation it comes from, ask people who consider themselves experts, and have them look at it. You try to put as much of the story together as you can. In the end, because of eBay, now everyone wants a certificate of authenticity, but as I point out to people: Who signed this certificate? As far as I'm concerned, no legit book dealer or autograph trader that I've ever known in my life would ever offer a certificate of authenticity. That's a warning bell right there, the mere offering of one. That's become a popular paradigm on eBay. It's what's allowed predators to be so successful and grow so large."

One of the dealers I met at the New York fair, Dan Gregory, of Between the Covers Books in Merchantville, New Jersey, worries about yet another problem he sees on eBay: fake dust jackets. Gregory is an expert in dust jackets and explained the phenomenon. Given that the cost of a first edition of *The Great Gatsby* without a dust jacket is $150 and one with can fetch $4,000, there's great incentive to print one yourself (possible with current technologies and a lot of savvy) or to swap jackets with a less valuable copy of the book.

"If I were a bad guy instead of a good guy, that's what I'd

be doing," said Gregory, who predicts that in ten or twenty years, when those who have found deals too good to be true on eBay decide to sell their collections, they'll find that indeed, those deals were too good to be true.

❧❧

ONE REASON Gilkey had been so difficult to catch was that he was not selling his stolen books on eBay or any other website. And that's one of the reasons his capture was so satisfying to Sanders. Shortly after he e-mailed his colleagues about Gilkey's arrest, Sanders went to San Francisco for that memorable California International Antiquarian Book Fair. As is typical for this fair, opening day drew thousands of collectors who, once through the front doors, were busy tracking down books. Even among this crowd of hungry collectors, and with a booth full of gems like the *Book of Mormon* and Kennedy's *The Strategy of Peace*, Sanders still couldn't keep his mind off Gilkey. For three years, he had kept after his colleagues both to report thefts and to be on the lookout for attempts to resell the stolen material, and nothing had come of it. They'd come so close, but they still hadn't nailed the "sumbitch," and not only was Gilkey out on bail, he was now paroled in San Francisco.

Since Sanders and Lopez decided not to post the mug shot or hang wanted posters of Gilkey around the fair (in order not to corrupt the identification process in a potential lineup), they were among only a handful of dealers who might recognize him.

So when Gilkey walked through the front door of the fair and immediately felt he was being watched, it may have been in his head. Still, he was determined to find someone who would buy one of the books he had brought because he needed to raise money for an attorney. He drifted from one dealer's booth to the next, admiring books, asking questions. At one of his favorite stops, the Heritage Book Shop booth, he admired Ayn Rand's *The Fountainhead*. He thought that one of the owners, Ben or Lou Weinstein, recognized him because, as he says, "I did business with him," Gilkey's euphemism for stealing. "I didn't take anything from him, though," he protested. "I had a taxi driver pick it up."

Gilkey tried to sell Heritage his stolen copy of *The Invisible Man*, by H. G. Wells, but they declined. He wanted at least $1,000, but they offered only $500. He also approached John Crichton of Brick Row Books, who was unaware that this was the man whose father had picked up *The Mayor of Casterbridge*. At Sumner and Stillman Rare Books, Gilkey ogled a first edition of George Orwell's *1984*, which was priced at about $2,000. At another booth, he was intrigued to learn from a dealer that author Lewis Carroll had invented the dust jacket.[1]

Gilkey had read that John Dunning, author of the best-selling Cliff Janeway rare book mystery series that had so inspired him, was speaking, but didn't see him at the fair. He would have liked to have asked Dunning for his autograph.

Gilkey told me that he did stop by Sanders's booth. He glanced at a number of titles by Wallace Stegner, whom he had never heard of, and saw books about Mormons, which he had absolutely no interest in, so he didn't linger. At the time, he had no idea that Sanders was the man who had set his capture in motion.

Despite the heightened awareness of several of the book-sellers and Gilkey's motivations to unload some of his stolen wares, no criminal activity was identified during the three-day fair.[2] No one reported any books missing, and no one noticed one man's peddling of suspicious items. It was the next month, on March 25, that Sanders received word that the activity had started up again. Gilkey had surfaced in San Francisco, attempting to buy books with bad checks. Sanders sent another e-mail to ABAA members:

> Earlier this afternoon he went to Tom Goldwasser's shop and attempted to buy several John Kendrick Bangs first editions. Be on lookout! Gilkey is 5'9'', 130 pounds, mid 30s, straight brown hair, rounded shoulders. He is described as soft spoken, clean shaven, casually dressed with windbreaker and cap. While in Goldwasser's shop

today, he was carrying newspapers, including a copy of Art
News. He said he had a collection of John Kendrick Bangs.
Also, another older man in shop may have been there to
distract. He was in his 50s, taller, 6', grayish hair.

Two days later, Sanders learned from Munson that Gilkey
had shown up in court without his attorney. The hearing had
to be postponed. Gilkey was set to go to court again, but
Munson said it would be six to twelve months before any
depositions. Due to standard delays in the court calendar,
Gilkey was free for up to another year.

A year of freedom following arrest and the payment of
bail. It was a formula for revenge. Even after having been
caught, and perhaps because of it, Gilkey was confident he
could now do whatever he wanted. The worst was behind
him. He was sure that after the year was up, a judge wouldn't
sentence him to more than a few months in prison, and that
was nothing, just a blip in his plans. For now, building the
collection was what mattered.

Less than a week after Sanders's e-mail message, on
April 1, Cynthia Davis Buffington of Philadelphia Rare Books
and Manuscripts wrote to Sanders:

Phone order today for $6500. American Express name:
Isser Gottlieb. Conversation felt right, authorization came
through. Caller said he wasn't sure the Oakland shipping

address was current card address. Said he'd just moved

from Savannah and gave me address there also. Googled

ship address: Hilton. Phone area code: san fran . . . I called

American Express. They said fraud.

Sanders had Buffington send a dummy package overnight to the address given by the caller. It was delivered to the Hilton Hotel the next morning, but no one showed up to pick it up. Gilkey hadn't made a reservation under a phony name, either. Munson and his officers had waited outside the hotel from ten A.M. to four P.M.

*We'll just have to wait for the next one,* he wrote Sanders.

A couple of weeks later, Sanders got word that Gilkey (who was not using an alias) was in Los Angeles, trying to sell a set of Winnie-the-Pooh books by A. A. Milne worth $9,500 for a price far below their value, first to William Dailey Rare Books, then to Heritage Book Shop. The books were: *When We Were Very Young,* 1925; *Winnie-the-Pooh,* 1926; *Now We Are Six,* 1927; and *The House at Pooh Corner,* 1928. Recognizing Gilkey's name from Sanders's e-mails, both stores contacted him. Dailey e-mailed that when Gilkey left his shop, he'd climbed into a Nissan with the license plate SHERBET. Sanders alerted the trade.

Dailey forwarded the address Gilkey had given them on Gateview Court to Sanders. *Anyone in San Francisco, please comment on address*, e-mailed Sanders, even though he assumed it was bogus.

Several people replied, and Sanders learned from Munson that the address was on Treasure Island, a man-made swath of land that sits in the middle of the bay between San Francisco and Oakland. A WPA project from the 1930s, the island was built with mud dredged from the Sacramento Delta, and its name was inspired by the gold that may have been buried in the soil. San Francisco's first airport was on Treasure Island, as were a military base and the site of the 1939 Golden Gate International Exposition, but many of its buildings are now empty. Nowadays, much of the island seems like a ghost town surrounded by water and the silhouettes of San Francisco, Marin County, and the East Bay. Few people live there.

That a book thief might be living—and possibly hiding his stash—on Treasure Island seemed storybook perfect, not only because it is the name of a famous, oft-collected book (exceptional first editions can go for over $30,000) but also because it's so evocative of the treasure hunt that book collecting often is.

Sanders thought it unlikely that Gilkey would have given anyone his correct address, but dutifully called Munson with it anyway.

"I hate to waste your time," he said. "I doubt this is any good."

Arnold Herr, a bookseller in L.A., was in fact reading Sanders's latest alert concerning Gilkey's attempts to sell the A. A. Milne books, when he looked up to see a man who resembled the photo of Gilkey. It was as if the bookseller had conjured the thief just by thinking about him. But there he was, approaching the counter. Herr steeled himself.[3]

"Nice shop you have here," said Gilkey. "I've got these four Winnie-the-Pooh books. Very nice condition. Any chance you're interested in buying them?"

Herr looked at the books, stalling for time. "Uh, I think I have a customer who may be interested," he said. "Why don't you call me in an hour or so, after I've had a chance to talk to her."

"Well," said Gilkey, "I'm checking out of my hotel at one or two o'clock, so I really need to take care of this soon."

No sooner had Gilkey spoken those words than they were reported to Sanders.

At Sanders's suggestion, Herr then called Dailey, who said there was no way to prove that the books were stolen. Herr then reached Gilkey at the Hyatt in West Hollywood, and Gilkey assured him he was still eager to sell. Herr told him that the potential customer was out of town for the weekend, but that he could reach her Monday. Gilkey gave Herr his cell phone number.

Twelve minutes later, Sanders received an e-mail from George Houle of Houle Books in L.A., saying that Gilkey had just left his shop with the Milne he had tried to sell. Gilkey had told Houle he was waiting for a taxi, but Houle watched him get into a dark car with no plates. Houle couldn't see the driver. The car had been parked a block away, even though there was plenty of parking in front of the store.

Sanders informed the ABAA of Gilkey's recent activities, noting that he was described as wearing a blue Caesars Palace jacket and tan trousers. He then suggested that Southern California dealers set up a phone tree to alert those who didn't have access to the ABAA e-mail list.

Late that night, at nearly eleven, Malcolm Bell from Bookfellows Fine and Rare Books, a non-ABAA bookseller who had received an alert by phone, wrote to Sanders:

> Unfortunately, I got info too late. Gilkey was here 4:00 Saturday, offering four Pooh's for $2000. I had no interest. His manner was pleasant and he was chatty. He appeared to me to be collector. He looked at our stock. Asked my wife to open science fiction case. He selected two: Shirley Jackson's Raising Demons, first edition $100, and Robert E. Howard's Conan the Barbarian first edition $200.
>
> He paid with check, presenting a passport and license

number for ID . We will deposit check on Monday with little
hope of it going through. He had a small rolling case and
made mention of traveling by plane.

The next morning, Bell e-mailed Sanders: *We've applied
for ABAA membership.*

❖ ❖

A FEW DAYS LATER, on April 24, Detective Ken Munson
struck gold. Search warrant in hand, he decided to investi-
gate the Treasure Island address Gilkey had provided. Munson rang the bell, but no one answered. He used a key he had
obtained from the apartment's management office, and
as soon as he opened the door, he knew he was in the
right place. The address was indeed Gilkey's, and every surface was covered in books. Moving through the dreary,
government-subsidized three-bedroom apartment, Munson
and his three accompanying officers found books in the
kitchen, on the bookshelf, in the bedroom, on counters, on
dining room chairs. Some of the oldest items were an illuminated leaf from a Book of Hours, circa 1480, encased in a
plastic sleeve; a land deed from 1831; and a signature of Andrew Jackson. Along with the books were coin collections,
stamps, documents, baseball cards, posters, and autographed
photographs. There were also books, advertisements, and

articles throughout the apartment related to these items and their value. The officers found what appeared to be shopping lists of book titles and authors. They also found receipts for hotels, and cards and papers with the names of auction houses and bookstores, several of which Munson recognized as having been victims of fraud within the past three years. Receipts for various hotels and travel documents were also among the goods. It appeared that both John Gilkey and his father, Walter Gilkey, were living in the apartment, and in John's bedroom they found a manila envelope with Saks Fifth Avenue credit receipts and pieces of paper with credit card holders, credit card numbers, and expiration dates handwritten on them.[4]

Munson took out his cell phone and, from John Gilkey's living room, placed a call to Ken Sanders.

Sanders couldn't believe what he was hearing. He wanted to jump on a plane, but he got Munson to describe the scene inside Gilkey's apartment.

"Can't you just box it all up, haul it off, and sort out the ownership later?" Sanders pleaded.

Munson explained that nothing could be removed without information indicating it was indeed stolen. Standing in front of a bookcase filled with what looked like valuable books, he asked Sanders for the names of any books he was sure were stolen.

Sanders scrambled to his computer for the theft reports

and worked as fast as he could. "Is there an *On the Road* by Jack Kerouac?" he asked.

Munson said yes.

"Grab it!" said Sanders. "What about a *Mayor of Casterbridge*?"

"Yes."

"And *Lord Jim*?"

"Yes."

And so it went. With Sanders's help, Munson was able to identify twenty-six stolen books in Gilkey's apartment that day. Sanders felt especially happy that the "trilogy of Kens" was able to recover L.A. bookseller Malcolm Bell's books, only three days after Gilkey had taken them. "That's got to be a record," said Sanders. But with no further proof of theft, the majority of the books were left behind.

Later that day, Gilkey returned to his apartment. As he approached the building, he noticed that the lid of one of his garbage cans had been removed and that the contents were strewn over the sidewalk. He had a hunch the police had been there. When he entered the apartment, he knew. He had given in to the temptation of keeping his books around him, indulging in their presence rather than hiding them in a storage facility he rented, and it was now his undoing.

The next day, Sanders e-mailed the trade.

It's with great pleasure to report that the San Jose high tech crimes unit raided Gilkey's apartment on Treasure Island. . . . I urgently need anyone who's lost a book from Gilkey or one of his aliases to contact me immediately!

The apt is a treasure trove of allegedly stolen books the detectives are packing up right now. Also autographs, coins, movie posters . . . Gilkey is still at large, expected to be arrested in near future.

Sanders closed the e-mail with his usual warning: *Govern Yourselves Accordingly.*

Over the next two days, Sanders's e-mail inbox was flooded with titles of stolen books and their identifying marks (torn pages, inscriptions, stains, etc.) from dealers around the country. There were also more e-mails from appreciative dealers. Florence Shay, of Chicago, wrote to the long-bearded Sanders: *You're the equal of Poirot, even though the facial hair is arranged differently.*

On April 24, Gilkey arrived in court for another hearing. When the judge heard from police what he had been up to in Los Angeles and San Francisco, his bail was raised to $200,000.

The question of Gilkey's partner, or partners, continued to goad the Kens. There was the driver of the car with the SHERBET license plates, and the older man who had been seen during several pickups. Gilkey usually said his father or brother or uncle or nephew would pick up the books, but how many of them were there? Were they really family members, or were they simply partners in crime? Sanders wrote to the ABAA members: *Munson's doing a photo lineup with Crichton.*

That day, Munson checked the registration for the SHER-BET car that Gilkey had been seen in. It belonged to Janet Colman, a woman in the movie poster business who owned Hollywood Poster Exchange. Not long after, through further investigating, Munson determined that the Ice Cream Lady, as Sanders called her, was innocent. Gilkey had sold a poster to her, and she had offered to drive him around. There was no connection between her and the thefts.

There was plenty of evidence to support the case against Gilkey, however. Munson found that every credit card holder whose number was used by Gilkey had been a customer at Saks, and that the phone numbers he gave various dealers matched the hotels where he had stayed or had the books delivered. At the Radisson Hotel in Brisbane, his telephone charges included calls to Lion Heart Autographs, Butterfield & Butterfield Auctioneers, R&R Enterprises (an auction house), and University Stamp Company (another auction house).

On April 30, Sanders wrote to Lopez that Gilkey was set to go to court the next week to be assigned a public defender—

that is, if he couldn't make bail or afford his own attorney. Munson hoped he would have a public defender, because there was a greater chance Gilkey would accept a plea bargain of three years. If not, he would be headed to a jury trial.

The next day, Munson and another officer went to Brick Row in San Francisco and showed owner Crichton six photos, one at a time. Gilkey's father, Walter, was Photo 2 (his driver's license photo). Crichton looked at each and said he believed that Walter was one of the first three photos, and when Munson showed him the photos again, he wasn't sure but narrowed it down to Photo 2 or Photo 3. On the last viewing, Crichton correctly identified the man who had picked up *The Mayor of Casterbridge* as Photo 2. Munson now had another positive ID. In his police reports, he added Gilkey's father's name. Walter had previously been charged only with possession of stolen property, but was now charged with his son's alleged crimes as well: "(S) John Gilkey and (S) Walter Gilkey should be charged with 182 PC—Conspiracy, 487 PC—Grand Theft, 530.5 PC—Identity Theft, 484 (g) PC—Theft of Access Card and 496 PC—Possession of Stolen Property."

From early July through September, Munson kept Sanders abreast of Gilkey's case. Gilkey did not opt for a public defender, and for the first several weeks, he repeatedly hired new attorneys, then fired them, delaying the process.[5] Finally, the deputy attorney general said he would listen to anything Gilkey had to say, but that he still had to plead guilty and accept a sentence of three years. If he did not accept this arrangement, the court would file the additional ten to twelve felonies, including those involving his father. Remembering that two years earlier his attorney had suggested he might benefit from a psychiatric evaluation, Gilkey tried that tack again, but the judge wasn't going for it, so he pleaded guilty. He also told the judge he wanted to appeal the decision, a tactic he thought would enable him to stay even longer in county jail, which was much more comfortable than state prison. The judge would hear nothing of it. She sent him to San Quentin.

Almost exactly a year after the sting, on February 24, 2004, Munson e-mailed Sanders to notify him that Gilkey had been shipped to state prison. *So while he appeals,* wrote Munson, *he can do it from somewhere not as pleasant as the county jail.*

So it was in San Quentin State Prison that Gilkey lived twenty-three hours a day in a cell,[6] imagining ways to win an appeal. Even if he were to lose it, he knew he would probably serve only half of his three-year sentence. Still, eighteen months seemed, as he put it, "an awfully long time to be behind bars for liking books." He spent those months sleeping most of the day so that he wouldn't have to deal with his fellow inmates, and lying awake at night, thinking about how unjust the world was and how deserving he was of a better life and more rare books. It was the point in a repeating cycle he'd lived through many times, yet it was no less powerful for its frequency. If anything, its repetition fomented a deep desire, once again, for getting even.

## ✤ 9 ✤

# Brick Row

A couple of months after Gilkey's 2005 release from prison, I met him in front of 49 Geary Street, a building that houses several art galleries and rare book stores in San Francisco. It was a September morning and he wore a bright white sweatshirt, pleated khakis, his beige leather sneakers, and the PGA baseball cap. He held a folder, on top of which lay a handwritten, numbered list, his to-do list for the day.

"So, how do you want to do this?" he asked.

The week before, he had agreed to let me tag along with him on one of his scouting trips, to learn how he selects books. I had suggested going to Goodwill, a frequent haunt of his now that he was persona non grata in most San Francisco rare book shops. Gilkey, though, wanted to take me to Brick Row, from which he stole *The Mayor of Casterbridge*. I tried to mask my disbelief and hoped he would think of another place.

"Are you sure?" I asked. "Wouldn't Goodwill work? Or, if not that, aren't there any other stores you can think of?"

Probably sensing my unease, he hesitated. "Maybe they'll recognize me," he said, but then he reconsidered. "On second thought, it won't be a problem."

At home, I e-mailed Sanders for his opinion: Would the owner, John Crichton, whom I had not yet met, be upset or angry that I'd knowingly accompanied a rare book thief into his store? I didn't relish dealing with the wrath of one of Gilkey's victims, however peripherally.

"Crichton's a good guy," Sanders assured me and gave me the impression that, as Gilkey had said, it wouldn't be a problem.

I was still wary, but too curious to walk away from an opportunity to see Gilkey in his element. What sort of person returns to the scene of his crime? So far, I had come to know Gilkey only through our private conversations. I still had no idea how he behaved out in the world, especially his idealized rare book world. He shared many characteristics of other collectors, but his thieving set him apart in ways that still confounded me: Was he amoral or mentally ill? How are such lines drawn, anyway? Accompanying Gilkey to Brick Row was an irresistible chance to be an eyewitness. Also, I had heard that the shop was well regarded among rare book collectors, and I wanted to see it firsthand. I had arranged to write a story about Gilkey and Sanders for *San Francisco Magazine*, so with the assignment in hand, I headed off to observe Gilkey as I had never seen him before.

Standing on the sidewalk in front of Brick Row, Gilkey said he would show me what he typically looks for and how he goes about it.

He did not appear to be apprehensive. I, on the other hand, was all nerves. I had no idea what Crichton might do when we walked in. This, at the very least, was going to be awkward.

We took the elevator to the second floor. The sign outside the elevator indicated that Brick Row Books was to the left, down the hall, but Gilkey headed to the right. I pointed to the sign, and he said that they must have moved. Later he noted with some satisfaction that Brick Row must not be doing very well these days because their old location, at the other end of the hall, was bigger.

We passed the rare book shop of John Windle, who had been helpful months earlier when I consulted him about the seventeenth-century German botanical text, the book that had captured my curiosity and led me to Gilkey and Sanders. I was sure Windle would recognize me and, I feared, also

Gilkey as we passed his shop, so I turned and looked the other way so that I wouldn't have to explain myself.

These are small, quiet shops, places where one customer is the norm, two is busy, and three feels bustling. Gilkey and I arrived at the door to Brick Row almost immediately. We walked in and faced two men, John Crichton, the owner, standing near the rear, and an employee sitting at a desk near the entrance. Did they recognize Gilkey? Would they call the police?

I wondered how Gilkey would react if they did. During a prior meeting, when I had asked him what he was up to, expecting to hear about books he was reading, or the research he was always doing, or his almost daily visits to the library, he reported a new problem.

"I just gotta be careful about what I say 'cause a couple of the book dealers are doing repeat complaints, tryin' to get me in trouble."

According to Gilkey, at his weekly parole meeting, his probation officer told him that an autograph dealer in New York named Roger Gross had alerted the police about a postcard he had spotted for sale on eBay. (In fact, Sanders had spotted it.) The postcard was signed by nineteenth-century composer Johannes Brahms, and Gilkey had stolen it from

Gross a few years earlier (but the police, not having proof—since Gross hadn't yet reported it missing—had returned it to Gilkey after the Treasure Island raid).

The week before his probation meeting, Gilkey had sold the Brahms postcard to a Colorado autograph dealer, Tod Mueller, but felt exempt from culpability. "I guess the guy [Roger Gross] was already reimbursed for the loss *and* he wanted his property back," Gilkey said to me, shaking his head in disbelief. In a bizarre, but what I was beginning to grasp as typical, distancing of himself from his crimes, he said, "Now, to me, I wasn't even involved. Gross wanted it from the guy who purchased it from me. Somehow my name came up."

*Somehow?* Once Gilkey had rid himself of the postcard, he felt that he should also be rid of all blame.

Inside Brick Row, natural light streamed through the windows, illuminating books sitting in cases along every wall and under windows, and on a graceful arc of shelves that ran through the middle of the shop. It was a quiet refuge from the city streets below, and if you ignored the computer and phone on Crichton's heavy oak desk, it could be a nineteenth-century bookshop. Thousands of majestic leather-bound books, many with gold lettering, caught the light as I walked by. Given Gilkey's Victorian library fantasies, I could see why he favored this shop, why he chose to bring me there. Unlike Sanders's shop in Salt Lake City, Brick Row was tidy and appeared highly ordered. I got the sense that only serious collectors would venture inside, in contrast to Sanders's shop, where collectors mingled with people in search of a good used paperback (he offered a selection at the back of the store). The doors of the locked bookcases on the right-hand wall near the entrance had metal screens in a crosshatch pattern that made deciphering titles a challenge. These cases contained some of Crichton's more valuable books. A filmmaker would do well to use Brick Row as a set for a gentleman's fine library. "More classier feel than some of the other bookstores that just rack them up in average bookcases," is how Gilkey had described it.

Crichton spoke from behind his desk. "May I help you?"

His question seemed to ask much more. He was looking hard at Gilkey.

"I'm not here to buy anything," said Gilkey congenially, "just to look around, if that's okay. We're just here to look."

No answer.

Crichton stood facing us. He was in his fifties, with white hair, a ruddy complexion, and clear blue eyes. He had an assured air and seemed to be the kind of person who rarely had the wool pulled over his eyes.

Gilkey referred to his list of the Modern Library's "100 Best Novels," and explained to me how he often looks for books on it. He pointed to the name Nathaniel Hawthorne.

"Do you have any Hawthorne?" Gilkey asked Crichton.

Crichton answered curtly, "No."

"I know he has one," Gilkey whispered to me.

His comment was a hint at his antagonism toward dealers, which he had made plain in our prior meetings. He'd argued that there was, in fact, widespread fraud among rare book sellers, fraud that made him not only blameless but also a victim.

One example Gilkey had cited was rebinding. Dealers, he explained, would remove the cover and title page from a second or later edition of a book, and then rebind it with a title page from a first edition that was in poor condition.

"They make it look like a first edition, first printing," he said. "That's part of the fraud they do. That's actually legal."

Later, I learned that there was nothing legal about this practice, but that it was not uncommon. The more expensive the book, the more likely it is that someone may have tampered with the binding. Such fraud is hardly new. In the eighteenth century, for example, facsimiles of pages, or "leaves," of ancient texts were sometimes created by hand, and to near-perfect effect. Of course, these efforts did not always go undetected, particularly when the pages were printed on eighteenth-century paper with an identifiable watermark. Even now, dealers come across pages of books that have been washed to give them a uniform appearance. Reputable dealers judiciously examine books for telltale signs of rebinding, but there are less upstanding dealers who don't. "You see a lot of that sort of thing on eBay," one dealer remarked, "but you'll never see it from an ABAA member. They'd be kicked out of the organization."

As we inched down Brick Row's bookshelves, Gilkey pointed to another book on his list. "Kurt Vonnegut," he said. "I'd like something from him, too. And D. H. Lawrence. He's also good."

Crichton looked stunned and turned his back to us, then turned around again to face Gilkey. A few seconds later, while Gilkey was explaining to me which books he might like to look for, Crichton asked, "What's your name?"

"John."

*John*—as though Crichton would be satisfied with a first name! I looked down at my notes while my heartbeat threatened to drown out everything around me.

"John what?"

"Gilkey."

Crichton waited a moment, glanced down at his desk, then looked up. He didn't take his eyes off us as Gilkey pointed to various books and whispered, as one does in a library or museum, informing me about additional authors he was interested in: Vladimir Nabokov, Willa Cather. He commented that he stays away from Bibles.

"And who are you?" Crichton asked me.

I explained that I was a journalist writing a story about book collectors. Crichton stared a moment. He seemed to be trying to decipher the situation. He handed me his business card and asked me to call him.

"For further interviews, if you'd like," he offered.

I couldn't wait to get out of there. I was desperate to explain myself to Crichton, and also to hear what he had to say in Gilkey's absence.

Surveying a row of ancient-looking tomes, resplendent with gilt titles, Gilkey said, "I think in the last ten years, a lot of rare books have just skyrocketed. If I was going to buy, I'd probably be looking for something like Salman Rushdie and Jack London and Booth Tarkington.

"See these cases," he said, pointing to the wall of locked cases with metal screens. "You can't really see through them." After trying to peer through, Gilkey said, "I think they have mostly nineteenth-century literature here, so no Kurt Vonnegut."

My tape recorder was running, and I took notes, but sporadically. I couldn't concentrate through the tension, and prayed the tape recorder was getting it all. Crichton came closer. I realized that he might be thinking that I, too, might be a thief, because as a reporter, I was asking too few questions. I was letting Gilkey go on, undirected.

"How is the shop organized?" I asked Crichton.

Curtly, he waved his hand in one direction. "These three or four tiers are nineteenth-century English literature." He waved it in another. "That's twentieth-century, English and American," he said. "And there's some other, more valuable first editions over here, organized the same way. Everything behind here is . . . uh . . . reference . . . Uh—sorry," he said, clearly distracted, "I'm right in the middle of doing several things today, so why don't you give me your number so I can call you. I do a lot of interviews with people."

In a tone that was somewhat louder, Gilkey then told me how at age nine he bought his first rare book, a first edition of *The Human Comedy* by William Saroyan, published in 1943, for $60, an unlikely story from the start. "And what happened was they actually cheated me," he said. "I found out six or seven years ago that it wasn't a first edition, first printing, which is how they sold it. So that's why I do a lot of research with bibliographies, check the details."

Not only was Gilkey's voice louder, but it had also taken on a bravado I had heard before, when he'd described thefts he'd gotten away with. He started in on another story, about buying a $3,500 book that was supposed to have been sent with a dust jacket, but wasn't, which made its value drop by half.

Gilkey had made a habit of sharing grievances with me during our meetings. He once told me that in his research, he had come across several companies that sell library books.

"I've been researching this at the library, because it coincides with some of my work. I was looking under certain titles and I kept coming up with 'missing,' 'missing.' The librarian said people are stealing books from the library."

Gilkey said this with indignation and explained his theory: "Book dealers are paying people to steal them. I think they're having someone go in and check the book out and not return it."

There may in fact be a few sleazy book dealers paying equally sleazy scouts to do dirty work in libraries, but I found no record of such activity, and libraries sometimes sell collections, which is how dealers often acquire them. If dealers are offered a book stamped with the mark of the library but not the "De-accessioned" stamp that should accompany it, they will contact the library to make sure the volume is not stolen. Gilkey's suggestion was in keeping with his general tendency to implicate anyone he might have victimized.

Gilkey continued to rail against the book trade throughout our meetings, and yet, as a reporter, I was in no position to contradict him. But sometimes it was hard to hold my tongue, as when Gilkey said, "It's a very frustrating thing for me, because I just wanted to check out a bunch of those first-edition books at the library, just out of curiosity, and they were missing."

*Just out of curiosity?* Did he consider me a fool?

"Have *you* ever taken a book from the library?" I asked.

Gilkey looked incredulous. "No," he said. "That would be stealing."

I had no idea what to say.

At Brick Row, the soft green carpet was lush, the kind of flooring that generously accepts your footsteps and makes them inaudible. It encourages quiet talk, but in an even louder voice, Gilkey went on to describe buying books at book fairs, only to discover later that he'd been cheated. It was obvious that these stories were for Crichton's ears as much as mine, and it pained me to listen.

We continued a few feet farther down the shelf.

"Theodore Dreiser," said Gilkey. "He's another one. He wrote *The Financier*, and they might have a copy." He scanned the nearest shelf.

My hands began to tremble. I dropped my pen.

Gilkey seemed to be enjoying himself. This was a dream of his, I realized, to show off rare books and broadcast his knowledge of them. "Here is my ideal world, here is what I know," he seemed to be saying to me. "And here is what I will one day own."

Gilkey walked a couple of steps to his right, where there were a few maps mounted on cardboard and covered in plastic. "A lot of stores also have maps, too. Here's one of San Francisco," he said, reaching for one, then adding in a raised voice, "What they do is, I guess they rip them out of books."

I avoided looking at Crichton so I wouldn't have to see his response.

Gilkey peered through the metal grate of one of the bookcases again. "Then there are certain books that an average collector will never be able to get, like Edgar Allan Poe. Books like that no one's going to be able to buy unless you're a top-tier collector, or your family happened to have one."

Crichton stared at us from his desk, where he stood. How much longer would Gilkey go on?

Gilkey and I had met many times over the past several months, and each time, after describing various tribulations, he would jump from one big idea to another. I had the sense he had been waiting a long time to talk to someone. One idea was related to the Modern Library's list of "100 Best Novels." He called the project "100 Books, 100 Paintings." He wanted to publish a book in which a scene from each of the one hundred novels would be illustrated. To keep his costs down, he was planning to hire just one artist. First he said he would read each book and give the artist instructions, but then he admitted that he might not read them all; he would just ask someone about them instead.

I was starting to comprehend just how curious and imaginative Gilkey was, but also how quickly his hunger for information was sated. This characteristic mirrored his collecting habits: he was not dedicated to one author or one period or one subject. As soon as he'd snagged a twentieth-century American mystery, he was on to a nineteenth-century English novel. He thieved across genres the way a distracted reader might peruse shelves in a library, running his finger along the spines, stopping at whatever caught his eye, then moving on.

I had tried turning the talk to work, which Gilkey had conspicuously omitted from our conversations. This absence was as baffling to me as his justifications of his crimes. His vision of the future never included a way to earn money. Again, hoping I might bring this omission to his attention, I asked about his plans for finding a job.

"Work?" asked Gilkey. "Actually, they do have an opening at a bookstore."

Of course.

Gesturing toward the locked cases near the entrance to Brick Row, Gilkey whispered, "I guess these are some of the really rare books in here." Then, much more audibly, probably so that Crichton would hear: "I think probably the *best* bookstore I ever went to was Heritage in L.A. They have like twenty of these cases. Sometimes I'd just go in the bookstore, when I was doing *that*," he said, referring to stealing books, "and I would call in an order, just pick it up. First, I'd take a quick look at the bibliography just to make sure I wasn't getting cheated. 'Cause I have been cheated several times by legitimate book dealers when I was a legitimate book buyer."

I was tempted to ask when he was ever a legitimate buyer, but didn't.

"And a lot of times dealers advertise that they won't take returns," continued Gilkey with more outrageous claims. "Those are the ones that belong to a specific organization. They have certain ethics that they have to follow. Couple times I bought books at a book fair. Then I called up the dealer and said, 'You said this was a first edition, and it wasn't,' but he said I couldn't return it. It was just the frustration of it. I guess I got a little upset trying to be a collector, buy things legitimately, and then I was getting cheated."

Gilkey sighed. At last, he had run out of steam. "So, I guess we're done here," he said.

I thanked Crichton and mumbled something about getting in touch soon, then headed out the door with my tape recorder, shoddy notes, and an immense sense of relief.

On the elevator ride down from Brick Row, I asked Gilkey, who spent more time in Union Square than I, where he recommended we have lunch. He suggested the café at Neiman Marcus, only about a block away. With high ceilings, glass walls, and pale wood and steel furniture, the café was a departure from our usual meeting place, the drab Café Fresco. Gilkey took a seat opposite me at the small table, slipped off his baseball cap, and ran a black plastic comb over the top of his head, following through with the palm of his hand. It wasn't an Elvis-like move executed with swagger, but something more tentative, self-conscious, an almost apologetic attempt to make himself presentable. It's a gesture you almost never see done anymore, especially by a fairly young man, and it served as a reminder to me that Gilkey is unlike anyone I know. Looking around, I was relieved that the café was patronized mostly by tourists and people who worked nearby. It was unlikely I would run into any friends and have to explain my companion. What would I say? "This is the thief I've been telling you about"?

Gilkey and I had established a routine, and our roles, interviewer, interviewee, were beginning to feel familiar. Still, there was a stilted formality to our conversations. Usually, I tried for an easy, friendly rapport with people I interviewed, but in

Gilkey's case I welcomed the defined borders that formality drew.

"I guess that was kinda tense," he said with a chuckle. He seemed invigorated by our trip to Brick Row. "I didn't know if he was going to call the police or something. Did you hear him whisper something in the back? He was probably telling the guy not to show me anything. But I wasn't doing anything wrong. That's why I told him I wasn't there to buy, just to look."

That Crichton would still be incensed about Gilkey's stealing from him hadn't occurred to him. He seemed happy that our trip to Brick Row had gone so well.

"He was kinda rude, but I guess kinda a gentleman, too. I was really surprised he remembered me. I've only met him like twice," said Gilkey, referring to a visit to Crichton's booth at the 2003 book fair in San Francisco and later, at Brick Row, when he tried to sell the Winnie-the-Pooh books. He hadn't considered that the crime he'd committed against Crichton might have cemented those two meetings in Crichton's memory.

"If it wasn't for you there," he added, "he probably would have called the police. Or harassed me . . . I did get a book from him, but that's why I told him just now that I was just looking. I got Thomas Hardy's *The Mayor of Casterbridge*, but he got it back."

Well, then, no harm done.

"The second time I went in there, I asked him if I could take a look at some books," said Gilkey, referring to the time he stopped by Crichton's shop to try to sell the Winnie-the-Pooh books in an effort to raise money for an attorney. "I knew these books were valuable and I knew I could get a couple thousand dollars out of him . . . so I went to him, and he immediately offers five hundred. There's no way. . . . They're worth close to ten thousand. . . . So I knew immediately the police were talking to him, otherwise he would have offered more. That gave it away. He was onto me."

What Gilkey failed to mention, but what I would later learn, was what happened when Crichton did not want to buy the Pooh books.[1]

Gilkey had asked, "Since you're not interested in these, is there something else you might want?"

"Yes," said Crichton. "In fact, I'm looking for a first-edition *Mayor of Casterbridge* in brown morocco." He was referring to the book Gilkey had stolen from him.

Gilkey, deadpan, didn't flinch. "No," he said. "I don't have one of those."

"Are you sure?" asked Crichton. "Because that is the *one* book I'm really looking for."

"I'm sure," said Gilkey, and he walked out.

---

"Those stories you told me back there," I said, referring to Gilkey's numerous claims that he'd been ripped off, "did you tell them for Crichton's benefit?"

To my surprise, Gilkey admitted that he had. "What goes around comes around. I was just evening the score."

The problem, as Gilkey saw it, was that he had evened the score too many times with too many dealers in the Bay Area. "I'm pretty much well known," said Gilkey. "I probably won't be able to go back in these stores, not in San Francisco. Probably L.A., New York. Just not San Francisco. I probably never can do this again. I mean, if I were to do crime like that, I never could do it again 'cause they know my method of operation. Even if somebody else does it, they'd think it was me."

Never again. Never again. Gilkey seemed to be trying to convince himself as vigorously as he was trying to assure me. I started to pack up my things, but he was reluctant to end our conversation.

"There's a book fair coming up in San Francisco," he said, referring to the annual public library sale. I thought he might be suggesting I go, but I didn't want to run into any dealers with him again. I suggested that instead we meet the following Wednesday. This time, I made sure the meeting would be at Goodwill.

## ❧ 10 ❦

# Not Giving Up

I called Crichton and explained why I had accompanied Gilkey to his store. He was gracious and understanding and told me that he had decided not to make a scene or throw Gilkey out because he didn't know who I was. As far as he knew, I had no idea Gilkey was a thief. Or maybe I wasn't a journalist but a fellow con artist scouting for a swindle. Crichton had decided to play it safe.

When I met with Crichton in his shop the next week, it was with a mixture of impatience and bemusement that he relayed the story of how Gilkey had stolen from him. He had since become more assiduous about all orders, not that any diligence is foolproof. "I've had guys come in here with three-piece suits," he said, "and the next thing you know they're conning you. You always have to be ready for someone, but I tend to trust someone until I have reason not to.

"I've been in the business for twenty-five years. . . . The books have become more valuable, so they're more vulnerable. Theft is very profitable. But I don't dwell on these guys," said Crichton. "Sanders dwells on them."

Back at my desk, I e-mailed Sanders to let him know what had happened at Brick Row. I assumed that with his love of stories, his curiosity about Gilkey, and his persistent fascination with book thieves, he would appreciate the news. As awkward as the trip to Brick Row had been for me, I was glad I'd gone.

Several hours later, shortly before I went to sleep, I checked my e-mail. There was a message from Sanders. He had been my guide through the world of collecting, and I was eager to read his reaction.

In formal, even language, not the sort of writing I was accustomed to receiving from Sanders, he spelled out how enraged he was by my trip to Brick Row. Despite my having consulted him before going, which he seemed to have forgotten, his disgust was plain. He closed the e-mail with a chiding request: *I don't want to hear about your sick games ever again.* It was a shutting down of communication. Sanders, the hero of this story, was turning out to be more intractable than Gilkey, the criminal. I lay awake much of the night, fearing that all my hard work had been for naught, that I had lost my story.

About a week after I received Sanders's e-mail, Gilkey walked into Acorn Books on Polk Street, a large bookstore with a selection of rare titles, and was recognized by employee Andrew Clark. Clark had worked at Brick Row in 2003 and had taken the phone order for *The Mayor of Casterbridge.* He approached Gilkey.[1]

"Please come this way," he said, leading Gilkey to the front counter.

"What's this about?" asked Gilkey.

Clark grabbed a camera from behind the counter. "You're going to have to leave," he said, "but first I'm going to take your picture."

Gilkey didn't budge, but instead looked into the camera. *Click.* "You can't make me leave," he said, agitated but not irate. He protested a little more, but eventually acquiesced. Whenever caught, he seems resigned to his fate, almost as though he has expected it.

Looking back, Gilkey considered the banishment absurd. "They don't know what's in my mind," he told me later. "I was there to actually pay for a bibliography." He thought that being ordered out of the store may have been a civil rights violation, and he intended to add that bookseller to the list of people he may sue.

In conceiving rationalizations, as with stealing books, Gilkey was unrelenting.

After a week or so, I called Sanders to hear his take on the Acorn Books incident and kept my fingers crossed, hoping he wouldn't rip into me. He must have either forgotten his anger or decided to forgive me, because he was cordial. He told me about another recent theft, which did not, apparently, involve Gilkey. It was one more example of a book thief walking away unpunished.

The story went like this: The staff of Borderlands Books in San Francisco had caught a man trying to sell them some choice first-edition science fiction books—*The Strange Case of Dr. Jekyll and Mr. Hyde*, *Beyond the Wall of Sleep*, and *Out of Space and Time*—which they recognized as having been recently stolen, along with ten others, from a science fiction bookseller in Portland, Oregon, named Bob Gavora. After consulting with Sanders, Gavora had spread the word to fellow science fiction booksellers about the theft, and Alan Beatts, owner of Borderlands Books, was one of them. He had worked in security at Tower Records for several years before becoming a bookseller,[2] and had a tougher, rougher attitude about theft than did many of his colleagues. He didn't just retrieve the books, he forced the alleged thief to sign a statement saying where and how he bought them (supposedly from a man on a street in Ashland, Oregon) and provide his driver's license and contact information. For a good half-hour, he scared the hell out of him. Shortly thereafter, the suspect mailed the remaining stolen books back to Gavora, along with a four-page letter insisting that he had not stolen them. Still, the district attorney general advised Gavora that without further proof that this was the thief, there wasn't much of a case, and Gavora declined to press charges.

A few months after Sanders told me this story, Gavora said he'd heard that the suspect had been arrested in Olympia, Washington, for attempting to sell a book to the same store from which it had been stolen, and was later, once again, released.[3]

"Of course" was Sanders's reaction to the update. Even when thieves take valuable books, their crimes are usually treated relatively lightly in court,[4] probably because the same traits that helped them get away with stealing books in the first place—politeness, education, solicitousness—also help them convince judges that they aren't the sort of people who would ever again do such a thing. One exception is the case of Daniel Spiegelman, the thief I'd heard about at the New York fair who'd stolen an astonishing variety of materials (a thirteenth-century textbook on Euclidean geometry; twenty-six presidential letters and documents; a 1493 edition of the Nuremberg Chronicle; twenty-six medieval, Renaissance, and early modern documents; and much more) from Columbia University and tried to sell them to dealer Sebastiaan Hesselink of the Netherlands.[5] Not all the items were recovered; some were sold, others damaged, many lost forever. The prosecution requested leniency, but instead, the judge imposed a stiff term and cited why:

> In callously stealing, mutilating, and destroying rare and unique elements of our common intellectual heritage, Spiegelman did not simply aim to divest Columbia of $1.3 million worth of physical property. He risked stunting, and probably stunted, the growth of human knowledge to the detriment of us all. By the very nature of the crime, it is impossible to know exactly what damage he has done. But this much is clear: this crime was quite different from the theft of cash equal to the appraised value of the materials stolen, because it deprived not only Columbia, but the world, of irreplaceable pieces of the past and the benefits of future scholarship.[6]

However moving this commentary on the nonmonetary value of books was, and as positive as it was in setting precedent for sentencing book thieves, it's unlikely to deter others, especially any like Gilkey. No matter how dire the punishment, it's virtually useless in thwarting crimes of passion.

Nor is the perceived futility of catching thieves much of

an obstacle for those who passionately want them behind bars. By the time Gavora contacted Sanders for advice about the theft of his books, Sanders had concluded his six-year term as security chair of the ABAA, but Gavora, knowing his reputation, chose to contact him, not his replacement. (As Sanders himself admits, "I do have a natural tendency whenever I get involved in something new to plunge into it, and I pretty much go off the deep end every single time. It's a pattern that's repeated itself throughout my life. [Pursuing thieves], it was a good thing; relationships with women, it tends to be a bad thing. I'm very unsuccessful at that.") And Sanders, ever eager to help catch a thief, gladly stepped back into his old role.

I was beginning to relate to Sanders in his obsessiveness. This rare book world had become almost all I thought about. My desk and bedside table were now crowded with books about people like Thomas Jefferson Fitzpatrick, a botany professor who bought so many books in the 1930s that his Nebraska house exceeded the building code maximum load.[7] When he died in 1952, at age eighty-three, it was on an army cot he used as a bed in his kitchen, surrounded by ninety tons of books. Might Gilkey steal that many if he could get away with it?

I was also devouring information on the much better known Thomas Jefferson, third president of the United States, who is legendary for his love of books.[8] (His family said that by the age of five, he had read all the books in his father's library. Even if the facts were stretched, the general idea wasn't.) When his earliest collection was destroyed by fire in 1770, he began replacing it with an even more expansive one. As the minister to France, he took time out to scour Parisian bookshops and ordered books from London and other European cities. In Jefferson's home library in Monticello, he grouped the books according to size: the smallest on the top shelves, the midsized in the middle, and the truly voluminous on the tall bottom shelves.

In 1814, when the British army burned the Congressional Library in Washington, Jefferson offered to sell his substantial collection of 6,700 volumes. The books were hauled in wagons from Monticello to Washington, where they became the foundation for the Library of Congress. Perhaps there were too many volumes to keep to the simple small-medium-large arrangement at home, because Jefferson proposed a classification scheme he adapted from Francis Bacon's *The Advancement of Learning*, in which books were organized within the broad categories of Memory, Reason, and Imagination, poetic divisions I'd like to see bookstores adopt today. It might take longer to find what you're looking for, but in browsing, who knows what you'd find.

The more I read through the stacks in my house about Thomas Jefferson, Thomas Jefferson Fitzpatrick, and the many other collectors who have written copiously about their beloved books, the more I thought about the role these men (and a few women) have played as preservers of cultural heritage. In the words of Wilmarth Sheldon Lewis, a collector who died in 1979, "Mad or sane, they salvage civilization."[9] I couldn't get enough of them.

Of course their salvaging of civilization hasn't always been popularly motivated. Some of these men have been remarkably selfish. One of the stories that kept me up late was that of Guglielmo Libri (1803–1869), one of the most highly regarded guardians of cultural heritage, who pilfered probably as much as he preserved.[10] Libri, an Italian count with a prophetic name from a family of old Tuscan nobility, was responsible for a loss of stunning proportions. A mathematician, journalist, teacher, adviser to the French government, and authority on the history of science, he moved easily in French, Italian, and English academic circles, and in 1841 was put in charge of cataloging historical manuscripts in France's public libraries. In this role, he was allowed in any room, at any hour, and often requested access through the night, ostensibly to conduct research uninterrupted. (When one librarian refused permission, Libri challenged him to a duel.) His reputation as a venerable scholar protected him long after suspicions rose about his thinning the collections. As the cataloger of the French libraries' vast holdings, he knew which manuscripts had not yet been recorded, and these proved irresistible to him. He was seen climbing ladders to reach the highest shelves, where the rarest works, often unbound and uncataloged, were stored. The man was not only voracious but cunning. He borrowed valuable editions of books and replaced them with less valuable copies. After removing libraries' markings by sanding the paper on which they were stamped, he would sell the originals at generous profits. Many of the manuscripts were priceless, ninety-three of them dating from before the twelfth century. In the end, his collection's worth was estimated at six hundred thousand francs (more than 1.5 million euros in today's world). He was finally caught in 1850, and sentenced to ten years' solitary confinement, after which he returned to Italy, where he lived for the rest of his life. I have serious doubts that this dueler for books lived that life without stealing more books.

❖ ❖

SHORTLY AFTER GILKEY told me about being kicked out of Acorn Books, he started talking about how impressed he was by the ways the San Francisco library protected its books. Apparently, one time he had simply wanted to make a photocopy from a book, but the librarian wouldn't let him. The only way I could imagine this happening was if Gilkey had attempted to take a book from a secure area, or if he had tried to leave the library with it. A few months later, in conversations with dealers about Gilkey, I must have mentioned my concern that he might someday steal from the library, because when I called his parole officer to confirm what Gilkey had told me about the terms of his parole, etc., he said he was not at liberty to discuss Gilkey but noted that at a recent parole hearing, with Gilkey present, someone had mentioned my concern that he might steal from the library. Word had traveled. I realized I had to be careful about what I said if I wanted Gilkey to continue talking to me. At that point, after months of interviews and research, I was elbow-deep in this story, and I had no intention of losing contact with either Gilkey or Sanders. We were all tenacious hunters—Gilkey for books, Sanders for thieves, and me for both their stories. What I had not anticipated was that my role would become more complicated. No longer the objective observer, I had stepped into the plot.

# This Call May Be
# Recorded or Monitored

When I was in Salt Lake City visiting Sanders, he told me a story about the time he visited author Wendell Berry, whom he admires greatly. Speaking in a cadence in keeping with both the rhythm of the place and the language of its people, he rendered a keen portrait not only of Berry and a Kentucky tobacco farm but also of himself.

"Wendell Berry has a place in the world and he knows it. I think in his youth he did wander away from the hills of Kentucky, but he came back home, and as he put it, 'Ever since then I've been growin' me a wilderness.' He invited me out there. . . .

"He's a working man, and it was harvest season, and he was helping the neighbors bring in the tobacco. . . . I'd never seen a tobacco plant in my life. Those things are monstrous! Huge aliens with leaves the size of this whole table and stalks almost as big around as this glass. [After work, harvesting tobacco,] we'd go back to his porch and watch the fireflies and sip bourbon. At six o'clock the next morning, do it all over again. Then Sunday, Wendell took me to his woods. . . . He has this sense of his place in the world and he practices what he preaches.

"I came back to Salt Lake feeling: This is my home, I was born here, I come from a long line of Mormon ancestors, but I don't feel that kind of kinship, I don't feel a part of this place, somehow. I feel like an expat in my own land. I don't feel that connection. I don't think I ever will."

Sanders may have felt disconnected from Salt Lake City, but it seemed to me that by tending his store, he had been growin' himself a wilderness of another kind, inhabited by an eclectic range of books and a continual stream of people who loved them. This was a world of his making, one he irrefutably belonged in. Sanders surely knows as much about his rows of books as Wendell does of his neighbor's rows of tobacco plants; when handed an old, obscure volume, he can sometimes sense its value in the same mysterious way a tobacco farmer might sense coming weather by catching certain scents in the air. Sitting with Sanders, listening to his stories, watching him help customers hunt down titles (*The Phantom Blooper* and "any Roman classics in Latin" were two requests that afternoon), it was I who was the outsider. I envied his lifelong attachment to this world perhaps as much as he envied Wendell Berry's.

My interest in Sanders's story, and Gilkey's, how they lived such different lives, and how they were intertwined, was now what possessed me. I was still trying to determine what made Gilkey so passionate about books, why he would put his freedom on the line for them, and why Sanders was so determined to catch him, why he would put the financial stability of his store on the line for it. So I made a goal to spend more time with each and to further explore the territory in which they overlapped: collecting.

Every collector, by definition, seems to be at least a bit obsessed, a little mad (one of my favorite books about collecting is called *A Gentle Madness*). To a collector, one is never enough, and when a collection is complete, another is imminent, if not already begun. The accumulating never ends. Even though Sanders says he doesn't collect anymore, he does admit that stocking his store is a form of vicarious collecting and that the stock is only part of his cache; he has a warehouse he refers to as "the catacombs," where thousands more books are stored. He sells books every day, but he buys even more. Gilkey is equally focused. Even when he isn't actively stealing books, he is researching them. Given the right circumstances, I wondered, how far might he or any obsessed collector go?

I found one answer in history. Don Vincente was a nineteenth-century Spanish monk who stole from the library of his Cistercian cloister in northeast Spain, as well as from several other ancient monasteries.[1] After disappearing for a time, he resurfaced as the owner of a remarkably well-stocked antiquarian book shop in Barcelona, where he had a reputation for buying more books than he sold, selling only those he considered the most pedestrian, and keeping the rarest for himself. One particular volume obsessed him: *Furs e ordinacions fetes par los gloriosos reys de Aragon als regnicols del regne de Valencia* (Edicts and Ordinances for Valencia), printed in 1482 by Lamberto Palmart, the first printer in Spain. In 1836, upon its owner's death, the book was offered at auction. It was thought to be the only existing copy, and Don Vincente was determined to acquire it. Although he offered all the money he owned, Augustino Patxot, a dealer whose shop was near Don Vincente's, outbid him. Don Vincente appeared to have lost his senses, mumbling threats in the street, and did not even take the *reales de consolación*, a small payment the highest bidder had to give to the next highest according to custom at Spanish auctions. Three nights later, Patxot's house went up in flames, and the next day his charred body was found. Soon, the bodies of nine learned men were also found, all of whom had been stabbed to death. Outbursts at the auction had made Don Vincente an obvious suspect. When his house was searched, the

just occurred to him that I might not perceive what he was telling me in ways that would benefit him. He seemed torn between his desire for recognition and his distrust of me. I admired his unconventional life, bold opinions, iconoclastic nature, artistic friends, enthralling stories, and dedication to his children and to his books, but the same wariness and suspicious nature that helped him in his work as a "biblio-dick" were now a barrier between him and me. I tried to reassure him that I was painting a positive portrait of him.

Gilkey, on the other hand, had not asked how I was going to portray him. Had he inquired, I would not yet have had an answer. *As crazy as Gilkey?* Sanders had asked. Was Gilkey crazy? If so, what was the diagnosis? With all the information I had collected, I was still lacking clear answers. Sanders and Gilkey had shared with me their histories, their desires, their motivations, but all this information did not add up to bold portraits sharply in focus.

Back home, I read in the newspaper that John Berendt, author of *Midnight in the Garden of Good and Evil*, was going to read that evening from his new book at a bookstore in San Francisco. I remembered that Gilkey had mentioned planning to attend. I considered going as well, but decided against it. I didn't want to endure another awkward encounter in public. Besides, Gilkey and I were scheduled to meet the following Wednesday at the Goodwill store on the corner of Mission and Van Ness streets in San Francisco.

I called Gilkey's cell phone to confirm our meeting, but he didn't answer, nor did he return my message. I called a second time, but again, no response. This was unusual, because he was always careful to be on time for every meeting and to notify me well in advance if he could not make it.

The next week, I received a collect call.

"Mrs. Bartlett?" said the only person other than telemarketers who calls me that. "This is John Gilkey."

He was calling me from a pay phone at Deuel Vocational Institution in Tracy, the prison where I had first interviewed him. He said he had been arrested in Modesto on the day I'd noted Berendt's reading, and explained that he had been put back in prison because of the Brahms postcard he sold.

"They offered me three and a half months, and I turned that down," he continued, explaining that he had instead been sentenced to nine and a half months. This was not the only time Gilkey had refused one sentence only to find himself, after protesting the unfairness of it, with a longer sentence. "I'm gonna go to the board to try to clear this up," he said, sounding resigned more than angry. "I'm innocent this time," he added. "That's the funny part."

Of course.

Gilkey said that after police raided his Treasure Island apartment, they returned to him several items they could not prove were stolen, including the Brahms postcard he had taken from Roger Gross. In his mind, this justified his contention that the items were not stolen.

"They gave it back to me," he said. "So what am I supposed to think?"

I was contemplating the convoluted logic of Gilkey's defense, when a recording interrupted our conversation: *This call may be recorded or monitored.*

When I told him I might visit him in prison, he was more than welcoming.

"Do I need to sign anything?" he asked.

I had decided to be more frank about my views of his stealing. I told him that I had spoken with dealers whose books he'd stolen, and that some said they hadn't had insurance, so they suffered the losses themselves.

"Well, if I were a better person . . . but I'm in jail right now, of course," he said, acknowledging that he might not be that better person. "I'd say that's the nature of the business. That's how I feel now. As a business owner I certainly wouldn't want to lose five hundred dollars. But if you open up a business, things like that are going to happen. 'Cause, like, a liquor store, it's probably gonna get robbed once a month. So if you want to open up a business, you gotta be prepared for stuff like that."

Stuff like that happens. That he made it happen was irrelevant to Gilkey. As he stated his views, his voice sounded the way it did when he told me about thefts he'd pulled off successfully. He spoke in short, staccato sentences, brimming with braggadocio, like a gangster in a 1940s movie. I couldn't help thinking that he was not connecting the dots, that he was not able to see how his criminal actions had put him where he stood, with a pay phone at his ear, guards at his back. I suppose I wanted him to make that connection. I asked him if he could imagine a life without books.

"Yeah, I can," he said. "I mean, I can't collect books unless people donate them to me."

Clearly, he considered actually buying them out of the question.

"Eventually," he admitted, "I think I should try to get another rare book. At this point I don't know how I would do it."

As robust as his powers of imagination may have been, he seemed incapable of considering a future devoid of rare books. Neither, it would seem, could he stop thinking of devious ways of getting them.

"To be honest," he said, "I did think of a criminal idea to get them. But I don't think it's feasible." He elaborated, "I was thinking something like insurance fraud," adding, as if in justification of his confession, "I am just being honest."

He continued, in spite of the frequent Big Brother–like reminder that the call might be monitored, revealing shifting impulses of dream, doubt, caution, and pride: "Insurance fraud to get all one hundred books [from the Modern Library's list] at one time. And that may or may not work. I probably won't do it. I mean, I did think of the idea."

I asked Gilkey if he thought what he had done was right or wrong.

"In terms of a percentage basis," he said, "it's not like I'm one hundred percent wrong. I'd say it's more like sixty percent wrong and forty percent right. I mean, sure, that's their business, book dealers, but they should make books more accessible to people that like them."

Seeming to anticipate my reaction to this, he added, "That's the kind of warped thinking I have." But just as quickly, he returned to his self-centered logic. "I mean, how am I supposed to build my collection unless I'm, like, this multimillionaire?"

Gilkey had a wish that he could not afford to grant himself, thus those who kept him from doing so, dealers, were to blame. What must it be like, I wondered, to view the world in such a way, to feel entitled to all one desired and to be able to justify to oneself any means of obtaining it? If this were truly how Gilkey perceived the world, and every conversation with him confirmed this feeling (I could not think of any reason for him to have presented these views to me as any sort of disguise; after all, they were not flattering), then perhaps he was mentally ill. He was aware that stealing books was illegal, and yet he continued to steal them, because he did not equate *illegal* with *wrong.* Was this a permanent state of mind, or could he change? He didn't seem to want to. Instead, he kept his mind on his collection, imagining how it would elevate his position in society. Gilkey would be regarded as a man of culture and erudition, just like the woman in the wealth management advertisement I had seen who was pictured leaving a rare book shop. Everywhere he looked—movies, television, books, advertisements, clothing catalogs—were images that confirmed our culture's reverence not for literature, per se, but for an accumulation of books as a sign that you belonged among gentility. Through his collection, Gilkey would occupy a revered place in an envied world. Maybe he was just a little more mad than the rest of them.

The recorded message interrupted again. *This call may be recorded or monitored.*

I asked Gilkey why he had left so many books out in the open in his apartment in Treasure Island, and he chuckled.

"Yeah . . . I was so stupid, I didn't pack them away and I left them in the bookcase. Cost me fifty thousand bucks in books. . . . I didn't think they would come and look."

Gilkey's honesty emboldened me. I asked him where the rest of the books were.

Apparently forgetting he had told me he didn't own any

books anymore, he said, "They're stored away. They [the police] took a lot of them . . . but I've still got some."

I asked if they were with his family, or perhaps in a storage facility.

Gilkey thought a moment. "Um . . . I've got them actually at an auction house, on hold. I keep changing venues. Keep thinking I'm going to sell them when all this boils over. I kinda pretend I'm gonna auction [them] off."

Gilkey said he had only a few minutes left to talk. He had told me that in 1994, he bought *Lolita* and *The Return of Sherlock Holmes* "on my own credit card."

I felt the pressure of time running out, so I challenged him again, reminding him that he said he didn't like to spend any of his own money.

"This is the thing," he said. "On the American Express card, they have a supplemental purchase plan. So I bought like fifteen thousand dollars' worth of items, and I only had to pay three hundred a month."

I was about to express my doubts about his willingness to make payments, when he rushed forward and confessed.

"I had another little plan behind that, so I essentially did get them free."

"How?" I asked.

"Well," he said sheepishly, "I told them I lost my American Express card, and that there were unauthorized charges on it."

In less than five minutes, Gilkey told me that he had bought a couple of rare books, that he had paid for them in monthly installments—and then that he had not paid a dime. Instead, he had claimed to American Express that the charges were not his.

"Okay," he said. "I guess they really want me off the phone now." We said good-bye.

I hung up and wondered if anyone else knew about his American Express scam. The credit card company? The police? Why did he tell me? Why wasn't he afraid I would notify anyone? Should I? Was I obligated to, legally? I was pleased he had given me this information, but I didn't want to be in the position of turning him in. I put off making any decisions until I could find out what my obligations were, even though I knew that what bothered me was a matter not only of legal duty but of ethical responsibility. Did I need to tell dealers? Would it do any good, since I had no idea where the books were? I decided it was best to talk to a lawyer before making any decisions.

❖ ❖

LATE THAT FALL, I visited Heldfond Book Gallery, one of Gilkey's victims. I had spoken with Erik Heldfond on the phone, and he suggested I meet with his wife, Lane, since she was the one who had dealt with Gilkey.

When I walked into the store, Lane was helping a couple of British men who appeared to be regulars. I didn't want to interrupt a possible sale, so I wandered around the store. Most of the books had gorgeous covers, and they sat facing out, rather than spine-to-spine, as if they knew their best sides. That day there was a spectacular first-edition *Thunderball* by Ian Fleming, a copy of *The Dial* with the first appearance of T. S. Eliot's *The Waste Land*, Richard Avedon's *In the American West*, and many first-edition children's books, such as *Green Eggs and Ham*, *Andersen's Fairy Tales*, *Elves and Fairies*, *Peter Pan and Wendy*. From her perch on a chair behind the counter, Lane glanced at me a couple of times with a suspicious look, and I wondered if she thought I might be a shoplifter. When the customers were gone, I approached the counter and introduced myself.

"Remind me what publication you're from," she said curtly, looking me up and down. Erik had told her I was working on a story about Gilkey, and she was clearly displeased. "Do you have a business card?"

I explained that I had left my cards in another bag, but that I was writing a story for *San Francisco Magazine*. She wrote down my name and phone number on a piece of scrap paper next to the cash register. I doubted she needed my number. The gesture seemed to be a way for her to inform me that she was no fool; she intended to look me up.

After Lane gave me the once-over, she reluctantly agreed

to talk to me. She recounted the story of Gilkey's placing the order, how he'd tried to disguise his voice by covering his mouth when he picked up the books, and how she had identified him in the online photo lineup. I knew most of the story already from talking with Detective Munson and Sanders. But they had not communicated to me one key detail: Lane Heldfond was angry. With few exceptions, dealers do not get rich from selling rare books; for most of them, a five-thousand-dollar loss is huge. Three years after the theft, she was still livid with Gilkey, and now it was clear that she was unhappy with me as well.

"What you're doing, is, well, it might be glorifying him," she said, noting the publicity that serial killer Charles Manson received: "Everyone knows who he is."

It was a bit of a stretch, I thought, to link Manson, the murderer, with Gilkey, the book thief, but I knew what she was getting at. They were criminals who received attention she thought unworthy for their deeds.

"This business is a labor of love," Lane said, and with her hand on her heart, she added, "It gets you here. I feel such anger for this guy."

Lane didn't want to talk anymore, so I put my notebook away. But as I was about to walk out the door, she stopped me.

"You know," she said, "we have really special books here. A lot of book-loving people who come in, they've never seen books like this, and chances are, they'll never see them again for the rest of their lives. We've worked hard for fifteen years, first buying eight-dollar books, hoping they'll go up, then eighty-dollar books, and so on. We've worked to build a gem of a shop, something unique. . . . We want these books to be with people who love them, people who pay for them, who appreciate them. . . . Gilkey makes me so angry. You feel violated. When he stole those books, he took them from me, from him," she said, indicating her husband, and then in a lowered voice, turning for a moment toward her daughter, a dark-eyed, dark-haired girl of nine or ten who was helping her dust the bookshelves, she said, "He took them from *her*."

What Heldfond said hit home, not only because of how she and her family had been personally affected by the thefts, but also in how she described what is on her shelves. Those books that we "may never see again for the rest of our lives" are more than just beautiful objects, and their physicality makes their contents seem more meaningful, somehow. Her rage was justified.

I had been thinking about the "thingness" of books ever since my first encounter with the *Kräutterbuch* and my book fair visit, but something Heldfond had said made me think, too, about the physical book's place, not just in larger history but in our own personal histories. This was an idea I couldn't get away from when, several months later, a friend of mine, Andy Kieffer, began extolling the virtues of his e-book. Andy and his wife had each bought an e-book shortly before moving to Guadalajara. They were glad they had, since it's nearly impossible to find books in English there, and the mail system is unreliable. He found he had no problem reading Chekhov's *The Seagull* or Stevenson's *Treasure Island* (two texts he recently purchased) on screen instead of between covers, and had now begun carrying the daily *New York Times*, several issues of *The New Yorker*, a language dictionary, and some trashy beach reading all on his device at once.

"I never know in advance what I'm going to want to read," he explained.

*Fine for him,* I thought. I still couldn't fathom why anyone who *does* have easy access to traditional books would make the switch. But then I thought of my teenaged children, both so accustomed to reading from their computers much of the day, not just instant messages and e-mails, but also long articles for homework. They will have no objection to reading e-books. At the same time, though, I think that may only strengthen their attachment to the physical books they do keep. One of my son's high school graduation presents, something I bought at the last minute, is a black pocket-sized copy of the U.S. Constitution (he's interested in history and law). Out of all his presents, a laptop for college included, it was this inexpensive, tiny book that my usually reserved son literally held to his heart, saying, "I'm going to keep this forever." And my daughter now has on her shelf my mother's (and once my grandmother's) copies of Lucy Maud Montgomery's *Anne of Green Gables*, *Anne of the Orchard*, and *Kilmeny of the Orchard*. "When I open those books and start reading, I like thinking about where they have been, who else has read them," she explained. "It's like they have more than one story to tell."

Physical artifacts carry memory and meaning, and this is as true of important historical texts as it is of cherished childhood books. Sitting in any library, surrounded by high shelves of books, I sense the profoundly rich history of scholarship as something real, and it's both humbling and inspiring. This manifestation of reality is true of other artifacts as well. We can read about the Holocaust or where Emily Dickinson wrote her "letter to the world" or where Jim Morrison is buried. We can view online photos of all these places. Still, each year, thousands of people visit Auschwitz, The Homestead, and Père Lachaise. I suppose our desire to be near books rises from a similar impulse; they root us in something larger than ourselves, something real. For this reason, I am sure that hardbound books will survive, even long after e-books have become popular. When I walk down the street and almost

# ✤·12·✤

# What More Could I Ask?

Since Gilkey, who was free once more, was now unwelcome at his favorite bookstores, he satisfied his need to be around books by visiting the library, which he did almost daily. He had decided to collect first editions of books by Nobel Prize winners, and the next time we met, he was happy to tell me that he had already found one, by Dario Fo, who won the prize in 1997. Gilkey had brought it along, a small, slim paperback with a plain red cover, which he handed to me. I noticed that on the back of the book there was what appeared to be a library sticker. When I asked him about it, he mumbled something about how he had bought it at a library sale in Modesto. While we continued to talk, he picked at the label, trying, I presumed, to remove it.

When I again asked Gilkey where he was storing his books, he said with a shrug and a knowing look, "Technically, I don't have any books." I was pretty sure he would have liked to tell me more, but he recognized this particular risk and with uncharacteristic caution was not willing to take it. Gilkey, who dreamed of being admired for his collection, was caught in a trap of his own making. As much as he wanted to show off his acquisitions, the very act would result in his losing them. Every book Gilkey added to his collection could now be only a private pleasure, not for anyone else's viewing, with one exception: me. I had become his audience of one. He couldn't or wouldn't tell me everything, nor show me all of his books, but he could show me small paperbacks that may or may not have been bought at a library sale and talk to me about their significance. The bigger "purchases," however, would remain in hiding, at least for the time being. Still, I had the sense that if I talked to Gilkey enough, some book-related gem would come out of it, and I was compelled to find it. I was hoping to dig up surprises as fervently as any book collector, so we set up another time to meet.

The discovery of valuable book treasures is not limited to out-of-the-way barns in New Hampshire. San Francisco dealer John Windle told me about going to an auction in London several years ago for the estate sale of a famous book collector whose books, furniture, and other items were up for bid. While reviewing the inventory, Windle opened a bureau drawer. Inside, unknown to anyone—not the auction house, nor his fellow dealers, nor the bidders—lay a copy of William Blake's illustrated *Book of Job*, an exquisite volume of twenty-one engravings. An exacting poet, artist, and printer, Blake has always been a favorite of collectors, and the *Book of Job* is one of his finest works.

"Tucked inside the *Book of Job*," noted Windle, "I found something even more valuable: a four-page broadside also by Blake, 'The Song of Liberty.'" Like a Russian matryoshka doll, one treasure lay within another, which hid inside another. The chest was priced about $2,000, and the *Book of Job* inside it was worth $100,000. The broadside hiding between its pages, "The Song of Liberty," hadn't been up for auction in forty years, so when Windle held it in his hands, he didn't know its value. He said he was conscious at that moment that no one else was aware of the broadside's existence. "Ninety percent of me wanted to put it in my pocket and go to lunch," he said. "But my conscience wouldn't let me." He informed the auction house of his finds. Three months later, "The Song of Liberty" sold for $25,000.

At our next meeting at Café Fresco, Gilkey told me about how his hunting was going. He had been researching Iris

Murdoch, whose book *Under the Net* was number ninety-five on the Modern Library's list of "100 Best Novels." He was particularly interested in her writings on existentialism. He said that he'd read Jean-Paul Sartre and Simone de Beauvoir, and his take on their philosophical leanings was personal.

"The way they can't differentiate between right and wrong," he said of existentialists. "Well, I've been thinking that could be me."

Gilkey told me he was hoping to visit Los Angeles for a book fair and Arizona for a horror book festival. I asked him if traveling wasn't awfully risky, suggesting that he might get caught violating the terms of his parole, but he dismissed capture as unlikely. And being around so many books would surely be a temptation too strong for him to resist, but when I asked him about it, he said, "Sometimes it's tempting to do it again, to be honest, but it's too much of a risk." But taking risks, gambling even on his freedom, had never been a deterrent.

Earlier, Gilkey had agreed to show me the pay phones he used to call in book orders, and now I suggested we visit one.

"As a matter of fact," he said, "this one here is pretty good."

Next to the café we'd met in so often, in the lobby of the

Crowne Plaza Hotel, stood one of his favorites. We gathered our things and walked over to it.

Gilkey opened the Yellow Pages, turned to the rare book pages, and ran his finger across the advertisements.

"Now, see, I've done some of these. . . . Looking back at it, I should have probably stayed away from that one," he said as his finger drifted down the page. "I've been to Kayo, I've been to Argonaut . . . Brick Row . . . Thomas Goldwasser. He almost got me in trouble. And here's Black Oak Books," he said, with his finger on the ad. "I'll just call them. It's toll-free."

I thought that perhaps I hadn't heard him correctly, that he was only going to pantomime a call, but a moment later he was actually punching in the numbers. With the receiver at his ear, waiting for someone to answer, he said to me, "I pretty much remember the phrases I used. I memorized them."

I watched, dumbfounded, grateful, and guilty.

"No one answered," he said as he hung up the phone. "It's a little irritating when they don't. When they would do that, later I would definitely make sure to get a book from them. I'd make it a priority."

He searched the ads again. "Brick Row?"

I couldn't help myself. "You're not really going to call them," I said.

"Maybe just to ask a question," he said. "Well, okay, maybe not. How about Jeffrey Thomas Fine and Rare Books?" he asked, referring to an ad. "Or Robert Dagg? Here's Moe's Books. They're actually quite good."

He settled on Serendipity Books in Berkeley, from which he'd stolen more than once, and dialed the number.

"Hello. I'm looking for a gift for a wedding. Do you have any rare books by Iris Murdoch? *Under the Net*, or anything else by Iris Murdoch? Or maybe something by J. P. Donleavy, like *The Ginger Man*?" (*The Ginger Man* was number ninety-nine on the Modern Library's list.)

While the person on the line searched for a Murdoch or Donleavy, Gilkey, not covering the receiver, said to me, "That's usually what I do, ask for a book I happen to be reading. Right now, she's checking. I think I told you, they've got thousands of books there."

Gilkey continued waiting. I continued watching.

"Only problem with this phone," he said to me, "is it doesn't take incoming calls. So I'd tell them I'm busy and don't take calls at work. Then later I'd call the store back to make sure the charge went through."

Gilkey waited another moment while the woman tried to find a book that might satisfy him. He grew impatient.

"See, for something like this, where they made me wait and wait and wait, I would definitely make sure they were next on the list."

The woman at Serendipity returned and must have asked for his phone number, because he read the number posted on the phone, and his name, because the next thing he said was, "Uh . . . Robert."

"I read on the Internet," he said to her, "that you specialize in Irish writers, especially James Joyce. Could you make a recommendation for a gift from an Irish writer? Oh, I think anything up to five thousand. Yeah, it's a wedding gift. Or if you have an autograph by James Joyce or Charles Dickens or . . . Okay, if you can just take a quick look. Okay, thank you."

I had heard this scenario before, from Sanders and from Gilkey's victims. They'd described for me Gilkey's voice while placing an order, his way of demonstrating a measure of book knowledge, his story that he was buying a gift. In tone and content, his enactment seemed almost a parody of itself. It was also going very smoothly. Even though Gilkey was not, I assumed, going to provide the dealer with a credit card number or hotel address, it was a deception I was witnessing, a half-crime—and I was half horrified, half fascinated.

Gilkey hung up the phone and gave me his take on the call, a blend of disdain for the dealer, pride for himself.

"See, that would have been perfect because the owner wasn't there," he said. "She probably wouldn't know the correct procedure. She doesn't even know where anything is. If I wanted it today, I probably would have done it. I'd have given her the credit card number. It would definitely go through. If it didn't go through, I'd have a spare one ready. I'd have three or four spares in my pocket. I'd order the book and say, 'What time do you close?' I'd say, 'Can you gift wrap it?' Then they'd stutter around and say, 'Uh, okay.' If they close at five, I'd get there around four-fifteen, four-thirty, take a look around, make sure there are no suspicious characters around. Then I'd go in there and say, 'I'm picking up a book for Robert,' and hopefully they'd have it ready. Sometimes they wouldn't have it ready, which would make me a little bit nervous. That's how stupid they were. They should have asked for the credit card. A few times they would run the number through when I got there. It didn't make any sense to me. But I signed it, and that's it. I didn't do anything suspicious or anything. I just said, 'Thank you.' I'd probably take a look at a couple more books and say, 'This is great. Thank you very much. I'll probably be back. You have a great collection.' And then I'd calmly walk out."

I nodded, balancing my notebook on the small shelf under the next pay phone, taking in just how replenished he appeared.

"Obviously," he said, "I'm not into it anymore. But that would have been the perfect opportunity."


Gilkey told me the story of another perfect opportunity as we left the Crowne Plaza and headed to one of his other favorite pay phones, a few blocks away in the Grand Hyatt. He and his father had taken a red-eye to New York and had themselves a few days of what he called "the good life," using stolen credit cards. The trip, said Gilkey, was "very, very successful." That's when he got the Winnie-the-Pooh books he later tried to sell, and a copy of *A Streetcar Named Desire* worth $3,000. Gilkey was careful to tell me that it was from "a shop" in the Waldorf-Astoria. "You couldn't believe how easy that one was," he boasted.

The third pickup in New York was, he said, "a funny story." He and his father were staying at the Hyatt near Madison Avenue, where there were several rare book stores. In a listing from one, which Gilkey declined to name, he had picked out a few selections, one of which was a series of travel books. Since he was having trouble deciding on one, he asked his father to choose. The elder Gilkey thought the travel books sounded appealing, so Gilkey called from a pay phone at the Hyatt and placed the order.

"So I get over there, and they were gift wrapping it," said Gilkey. "It turns out it's a seventeen-volume set. It must have weighed like seventy-five pounds. I had to carry it all the way back to the hotel." He said he didn't take a taxi because he didn't want to spend the money. "Very strenuous," he went on. "I had to keep taking breaks. . . . I kept trudging along, trudging along."

Did anyone know about this theft? Did Sanders? The

ABAA? When I asked Gilkey which store he got it from, he said, "I better not say." I heard this response more often now, because he was, in fact, confessing crimes more frequently. He seemed to be growing more trusting of me, and I hoped that he would eventually tell me where the books were stashed.

In addition to lining his suitcases with rare books and a handful of other collectibles, Gilkey said he and his father spent their time in New York "eating hundred-dollar meals, visiting the Empire State Building, and walking around Greenwich Village. We were eating like kings. I said to my dad, 'I guarantee you everything, the hotels, the meals, will be free. I guarantee you.'"

The trip was an inspiration.

"That's what I wanted to do," said Gilkey, "plan trips to other cities, especially because New York was amazing. Nothing went wrong."

Until their return. Gilkey and his father boarded the plane with suitcases full of loot, but after they arrived in San Francisco, Gilkey discovered that someone had taken his luggage.

"That was the worst thing that could have happened," he said. "All those thousands of dollars' worth of books."

A passenger from San Mateo had the same model of Hartmann luggage, and within hours he had returned Gilkey's bag. In spite of that experience, as Gilkey relayed the story of his trip to New York, it was clear that it was one of his fondest memories.

"That's what I wanted to do. Go to a city, get free hotels, free plane tickets. New York worked out perfectly. I had eighty to ninety credit slips, and I could get one thousand, two thousand, three thousand a slip at least. . . . If you like getting stuff for free, it was the perfect trip. I didn't feel guilty. Free vacation, free meals, free books. I was excited. I was gonna go mobile from city to city. New York, that was the test run. New York was the future of what I was going to do, because what more could I ask?"

## ❖ 13 ❖

# And Look: More Books!

After our tour of Union Square's finest phone booths, I didn't hear a thing from Gilkey for several weeks. While wondering if he had been caught stealing and was back in prison again, I kept busy. Once, when my daughter was looking for a costume at Goodwill, I drifted over to the bookshelves. This is the type of place where it's still possible to find a treasure, however unlikely. But maybe I would be lucky. Collector Joseph Serrano had told me about two of his recent finds there: a signed first-edition Willie Mays autobiography for $2.49 (he later saw two copies online, unsigned, priced at $400 each) and a first-edition *Booked to Die*, the book collector mystery by John Dunning (which Gilkey happened to read in prison), for $3.49 (Serrano estimates it's worth around $400 to $500). I went straight for a couple of "high spots," the Stephen Kings: no first editions. No *Tarzan*s, which I had heard were very valuable, either. As far as I could tell, there wasn't much of anything besides bedraggled airport paperbacks and stained cookbooks. I ran my eyes down one shelf, then another, scanning for hardbacks. Not a first edition among them. There were more bookshelves behind me, but unlike the scowling man in a darkly stained parka next to me, who was diligently searching for something (first editions?), I was ready to give up. I thought of Gilkey, who had been to that Goodwill before, and couldn't grasp how he or anyone else could keep up the search when it yielded so little. When I returned to the crowded racks of tulle and velveteen skirts my daughter was digging through, I was ready to go. She had had just as scant luck as I had, so we left empty-handed. As we walked out, I saw that the same man was still hunting among the books, building a small stack of them on the floor. What had I missed?

The next week, several times, I called the California inmate locator service to see if Gilkey was back in prison, but he wasn't. I called his mother's house, where his sister Tina answered the phone and told me she didn't know where he was. But I knew from Gilkey that the two of them were in frequent contact; I doubted she was telling me the truth.

Eventually, Gilkey called me and agreed to meet again, suggesting the Olive Garden in the Stonestown Shopping

Center. Over a pizza, Gilkey explained that because he had stopped going to his weekly parole meetings, he was now a fugitive, a "parolee at large," but he couldn't have been happier. He had bought a new laptop, which he showed me, and said he was taking classes at "a nearby college" that he was reluctant to name because he wanted his whereabouts kept secret. He told me he was enrolled in a class on the philosophy of Nietzsche, whom he had mentioned as an interest before, and was particularly taken with what he described as Nietzsche's idea that if a law or system is unjust, to break it down, to go against it, is not wrong. Apparently, the unfair system Gilkey had in mind was one under which he cannot afford what he wants while others can. There are books that cost more than Gilkey can pay, or wants to pay, so he steals them. It's a correction to the system.

Gilkey said he had a part-time job at the waterfront, but wouldn't give me any details. Living off a part-time job in an expensive city like San Francisco while staying in a hotel, however fleabag-ish, is no easy feat. I asked him what he was living on.

"I spent eighteen dollars yesterday," he said. "Then I got a Lotto ticket and won nineteen, so I actually finished ahead. . . . I figure I've got good luck now. It's time for a jackpot." He was full of energy and optimism. "What a story that would be! I win a hundred million dollars in the lottery and buy a rare book shop."

I had the sense he was offering me an ending to the book I had told him I was working on. It would not be the first time he had done this, nor would it be the last. The next time we met, he said, "You know, I've been thinking that by the time you're done with the book, maybe I'll have read all the one hundred best novels, and maybe I'll hire an artist to do the work, and I'll have a show. That would be a good way to finish it."

After giving that idea some thought, he added, "Unless I do something bad or something . . . but I don't think so."

"Have you been in any trouble lately?" I asked.

"No," he said, "I haven't had time."

❖❖

WHILE GILKEY WAS still on parole and living, as far as I knew, in a cheap motel in San Francisco, I drove to his family's house in Modesto to meet his mother, Cora, and sister Tina, a meeting he had helped arrange.

The Gilkeys live in a neighborhood of ranch-style houses with modest lawns bordered by rows of tall liquidambar trees shedding piles of leaves onto the sidewalks. It seems like the kind of town that thirty years ago rang with the sounds of bicycle bells and hollering mothers. I walked through the front door and into the dim living room, where every corner, wall, table, and shelf was hectic with collections. In one corner sat brass candlesticks, in another, English porcelain, "not like the cheap Chinese knockoffs," Gilkey's mother pointed out. There were Filipino fabrics, silver spoons, dolls from around the world, Norman Rockwell plates, salt and pepper shakers. Gilkey had said that his mother wasn't a big collector, but I doubt he had been trying to hide the fact; it had simply never occurred to him to think of her that way. To amass large quantities of similar objects, to collect, was like sitting down to dinner in his family: one didn't stop to take notice of something so natural.

Cora was a petite Filipino woman in her eighties with clear brown eyes and the slender, unlined hands of someone much younger. Her hearing was going, and her voice faltered, but her intellect and memory were sharp. After inviting me to take a seat on a dark leather couch that took up much of the room, she told me about how she had met her husband, the father of their eight children, in Okinawa while he was a serviceman, how they had moved to Sacramento, then there, to the house in Modesto, where collections of objects multiplied alongside their growing family.

"I got a lot of antique cups," she said in slightly broken English, pointing to a collection as she led me around the house. "And bells, brass, books, clocks. John says it will be worth something. . . . Here's a collection of cameos. John says to me, 'Don't sell it now.' . . . I love collecting Chinese engraved silver. Hummels. That's English, too. You go in the store, they don't look like that anymore. John gave this to me, a candle. And that, he gave that to me," she said, pointing to a brass candlestick. "You see all those angels there? John buy me all those angels. I got a lot of things. I told them [John and Tina], 'Don't let the others [siblings] get them.' When I'm gone, it's got to be divvied. But now they [the siblings] don't even come see me. . . . One of my daughters already grab a whole station wagon and fill it with my old hats. Patricia did that."

"My mom had these old hats from the sixties," Tina explained.

"I said to Patricia," remembered Cora, "'Help yourself with this hat,' but she took all of them."

We walked into the family room. "You see: books, books, books," said Cora. "All those are Franklin Mint books up above there. *Crimes and Punishment*. The old crimes, the old cases. Down below, piles of books down there. A lot of them are his, wrapped in plastic," she said of her son. "And there is his metal detector to find coins."

When we sat down to talk, Cora was eager to tell me about John. When she recalled him as a boy, she laughed. "He created stories and then just talked from his head!" she said. "And he loves to read. He can finish a whole book in one day or one night. . . . He has so many different collections and movie posters. He orders it, buys it, and knows he's gonna make a profit. So he makes money." She was awash in maternal pride. "You seen him lately? Oh! He's big. And well built. And one thing about him, of all my boys, he's the one with the real good posture. Always straight. My other sons, they don't have that."

Tina sat in an armchair at a distance from Cora and me, and seemed to be weighing whether or not she should join the conversation. Even with barely perceptible Asian features, like her brother, she strongly resembled their mother. Eventually, she told me how her brother liked to playact as a young boy. He would stand there, in the living room, make up stories for the family and tape them. Echoing her mother, she said, "They were often funny."

When I broached the subject of Gilkey's thieving, however, the laughing stopped. I asked how they thought he had gotten into so much trouble with the law, and Cora tried to convince me that he had been wronged.

"I mean, it's innocent. Maybe he was just wandering around or looking around with the book, and he must have forgot about it, and then he got caught," she said.

I wondered whether she was deluded about her son's criminal activities or was trying to delude me.

"His father," said Cora, her eyes darting in Tina's direction, "I think it was his influence." She nodded toward Tina, waiting for her daughter's agreement, but Tina was having nothing to do with this line of speculation. Cora went on. She suggested John's father's desire to live profligately influenced him, in fact forced him into trouble with the law. She looked again to Tina for confirmation, but Tina shook her head in disagreement. Cora then explained how when her husband left her, he took then nineteen-year-old John with him.

"I understand what his father deprived me of," Cora said sadly. "My youngest."

It was the one theft she did not shellac with misunderstood intentions.

If Cora or Tina had aided Gilkey with his stealing, they were not saying. I knew from my reading, though, that book thieves have often enlisted the help of family members. In one case, in Denmark in 2003, Copenhagen police found a trove of rare books, documents, and maps in the basement of a sixty-eight-year-old woman. She was the widow of a philologist who had worked in the Danish Royal Library's Oriental Collection. Between the late 1960s and 1978, it turned out, he had moved books off the library's shelves and onto his own. Police grew suspicious of the woman, her son, and her daughter-in-law when they attempted to sell several books, including the only existing copy of a 1517 volume belonging to the Royal Library, through Christie's in London.

Among the books stolen were works by John Milton, Martin Luther, Immanuel Kant, and the astronomer Tycho Brahe. At the time of the theft announcement in 2003, only 1,800 of the 3,200 missing books had been recovered, and at least a hundred had already been auctioned, including a first edition of Thomas More's *Utopia*, which sold for the equivalent of $244,500.[1]

Cora and Tina asked if I'd like to see some photos of Gilkey when he was young. They were organized somewhat randomly, so that a photo of Gilkey at age six might be next to one when he was a teen, opposite a page of older siblings' baby pictures. The pastel sixties mingled with the round-cornered seventies and flat-finished eighties.

"Do you want to see his father's picture?" Cora asked. She led me to the hallway, papered with portraits of their large family. The resemblance between John and his father was faint. His father had a lighter complexion, a fuller face. Cora and Tina showed me through the rest of the house. They pointed out some of Gilkey's prized possessions, including an oil painting of flowers.

"John wanted to make sure you saw that," said Cora, "so we put it up here."

So Gilkey had been setting the stage for my arrival. He

wanted me to see him as someone who appreciated the finer things in life.

We turned a corner in the narrow hallway. "This is John's room," said Cora. "Come inside. And look at these books here!"

Tina joined us. She held up a slick new coffee-table book on wine that sat on his dresser atop several other large new books.

I looked around and felt urgently that I shouldn't be there, in Gilkey's bedroom. His shoes were neatly lined up on the floor and artwork he had collected hung on the walls. Ceramic frogs, which they told me he had also collected for years, sat on his shelves. I made a move to leave, but his mother motioned toward the closet, which she opened.

"See how he keeps his things? Neat," she said. "And look, more books!"

Yes, more books. Stacks and stacks of them below and above the jackets, shirts, and pants that hung from the rod. Their spines faced the back of the closet, as if in hiding. This seemed the most private, most intimate corner of Gilkey's room, but instead of looking inside to see if I recognized any of the books he had stolen, I turned away. It was like being invited to view a ghastly scar, something awful but riveting. I was afraid of what I would find if I drew the books from the pile, what degree of crime, and what responsibility I might bear in knowing the books were there. Later, I would curse my lack of courage.

❖❖

IN DECEMBER, I met Gilkey at Café Fresco. The interview didn't last long. I had a few questions, some facts to confirm, but soon thereafter, a janitor plodded by with her roaring vacuum cleaner. The noise made audiotaping impossible, so I suggested we end the interview and meet again soon. We both started to pack up, and I turned off my tape recorder. Gilkey held up a paperback to show me.

"I checked this out of the library," he said over the drone of the vacuum, "so that they wouldn't notice a pattern."

I didn't recognize the title. I also didn't understand. "What do you mean?" I asked.

"I usually check out classics," he said.

"And?" I asked, still confused.

"See," he said, "I took three dust jackets off classics, you know, to send to their authors for autographs."

I was no longer confused.

"And a map," he added. "I cut one out of a book."

So much for not stealing from the library.

It was bound to happen. Imagine a jewel thief walking into Tiffany's and having all but the most valuable diamonds, sapphires, and emeralds sitting on velvet-lined trays out in the open. So it must be for a book thief walking into a library, especially since first editions can still be found in the open stacks.

When Gilkey told me about taking a map and dust jackets from the library, it was the first time he had confessed recent thefts to me—the others he'd pulled off years before. I assumed the dust jackets were not valuable, but what if I was mistaken? And what about the map? I had read about a New England map expert who had been charged with slicing millions of dollars' worth of ancient maps from libraries' collections. I doubted that Gilkey's nicked map was from a very valuable book, but again, what if I was wrong? Was this the kind of treasure I had been hoping to uncover? I wasn't sure what to do with it. I hadn't expected to take on the role of confessor, and I worried about the implications. Was I obligated to inform the police? What about the library? And which library? If I decided not to share this information yet, how would librarians and book dealers respond once they found out?

I consulted a couple of friends who are lawyers. After providing the caveat that they weren't criminal attorneys, they told me they were fairly sure that I had no legal obligation to inform authorities unless the crimes had or would physically endanger someone. Later, my literary agent's attorney echoed their opinions.

But what about ethical responsibility? The difference between the two was as blurry as my role, which had shifted from observer to participant in Gilkey's story. Did I owe this information to dealers, who had been so helpful with my research? But if I notified them of these thefts, wouldn't Gilkey keep all future and possibly more significant thefts from me? Furthermore, would he then never tell me where the misbegotten books were stashed? I found myself teetering between selfishness and benevolence: either reveal the secrets Gilkey had shared with me, probably losing access to him and possibly sending him to jail, or keep them to myself and be unjust to his victims. I tried to reassure myself that such consequences were not directly my responsibility.

Two months later, still undecided about what to do with this information, I called the FBI. I read that they had been involved in cases of rare book theft and I wanted to learn how many they pursued annually, which types of cases they took on, what sorts of trends they encountered, and so on. I was granted a telephone interview with Bonnie Magness-Gardiner, who heads the Art Crime Team responsible for rare book theft investigations. I explained what I was interested in and why. She was not able to provide me with statistics regarding the total number of rare book thefts in recent years, but said that the agency became interested in cases involving interstate transportation of stolen books worth over $5,000 that were uniquely identifiable.

"Then," she said, "it *could* become a matter for the FBI," adding, "but there's a five-year statute of limitations."

I remembered the $9,500 set of travel books Gilkey stole in New York and, crossing state lines, brought into California.

"You'd tell me," said the FBI agent, "if the book thief had stolen anything, right?"

"Oh, yes," I said, trying to sound convincing, "Of course."

As soon as I got off the phone, I dug through my notes. When had Gilkey stolen the set? I couldn't remember. And when had he told me? Had I waited too long to notify the police? Or now the FBI? Frantically, I flipped through thick binders of transcripts.

I dug and dug, and eventually I found it.

Gilkey had stolen the books in May of 2001, and had first informed me in September 2006, a little over five years after the fact. I was clear. But I was also stuck on the fact that Gilkey had told me of the theft just four months after the period of time in which he could have been prosecuted for it ended, even though we had been meeting for almost two years. Was he shrewd or, once again, just plain lucky?

# The Devil's Walk

During a trip to New York, I visited the Morgan Library and Museum. I had read about J. P. Morgan's private collection and wanted to see it up close. I was also eager to see a new exhibit, *Federico da Montefeltro and His Library*. Formed in the fifteenth century, his was the richest Italian Renaissance library to be owned by a single private collector.[1] It usually resides in the Vatican, but several prized pieces from the collection were on loan to the Morgan. Montefeltro, the illegitimate son of a count, had soldiered and studied his way to the lofty position of duke. Judging from what I saw and read, he probably cherished his books, but without doubt he loved displaying them for others. He had housed

the library near the entrance of his palace in Urbino, allow-
ing his books to be admired by many, even if only a few had
the privilege of actually reading them. He was also in the
habit of showing off his two-volume Bible, which according
to one scholar served to "proclaim his identity as a Christian
humanist prince."[2] Mere ownership as evidence of identity—
Gilkey would, no doubt, agree. The exhibit was on display in
a small gallery where the walls were hung with fine portraits,
and where glass cases held six-hundred-year-old manuscripts
and illuminations, but I found the most intriguing pieces to
be the large digital reproductions of several wood panels the
duke had ordered for his *studiolo*. Made of intricate inlay,
these wooden trompe l'oeils were realistic depictions of
cabinets with shelves full of books and musical and scientific
objects: an astrolabe, a mechanical clock, an organ, a clavi-
chord. Each was symbolic individually, and collectively they
formed a tableau of the duke's erudition and culture. While
Montefeltro was an impressive man of means and power and
Gilkey is not, standing in that small gallery, I couldn't help
wondering if either of them would have collected books if
they hadn't had an audience to appreciate them—or in
Gilkey's case, dreams of a future audience. In this and many
other respects, I came to understand that Gilkey is typical of
many book collectors. It is his crimes and his unwavering,
narcissistic justification of them that sets him apart.

Gilkey had spent that summer in prison for violating parole (police finally caught up with him at his mother's house), and in the fall of 2007, when he got out, we met a few more times. I wanted to ask him a question that had dogged me for months, a simple one to determine how knowledgeable and calculating, versus just plain lucky, he had been during his most active spree: Had he known that by stealing from different states, different counties, different police jurisdictions, he had made it more difficult for the court to convict him?

"It did?" he asked, puzzled. He considered the fact for a moment. "Oh yes, I did know."

He was a lucky man.

When I asked if he'd been aware of the FBI's five-year limit on pursuing stolen books, which meant that the crimes he committed could no longer be prosecuted, he was equally surprised.

Gilkey was lucky for yet another reason, although it took me some time to see it. As much as his passion wreaked havoc in his life, it gave shape and purpose to it. Often, when I told people his story, they would say, *How sad.* Here was a man who seemingly could not help himself from the very act that would put him in prison. I came to disagree. Such single-minded wanting is a lot like never-satisfied lust, a dream that won't die, and working toward achieving it can give tremendous pleasure. While Gilkey had told me he was depressed in prison and said he would never want to go back, I began to see his "frequent flyer" status (as one prison official referred to it) as perhaps he saw it: the price he had to pay. Some pay for their success with soaring blood pressure or dissolved marriages. He paid with jail time. To me, Gilkey had come to seem a happy man with goals, ambition, and some measure of success. His only sacrifice was a series of forced pauses on the way to realizing his dream.

One of the last times we met, as if feeling the urgency of time running out, Gilkey offered another idea for his future.

"I could have a T-shirt made that says, 'Will Work for Rare Books,'" he said. "There could be a picture of me wearing it over a suit. That might be good to include in your book."

That was not all.

"I had a couple notes here. I was thinking maybe at the end of the book . . . and I think it's a perfect ending, if the people who read it want to donate a book to me to keep me out of jail or something. I was thinking of something cheesy like that."

And then, "What do you think about bobble heads? Of famous writers? I've been doing research on copyright, and I thought maybe a limited edition of, like, a thousand bobble heads. I'd sell the books with them."

He was also hoping to visit ghost towns in New Mexico with a video camera and a metal detector. "I'd talk about the history a little and then try to search for treasure," he said. He would record his experiences and broadcast them on the Internet.

He was thinking about publishing books with expired copyrights now in the public domain. He speculated that Booth Tarkington's *Magnificent Ambersons* might be such a book, and if so, he'd print five hundred and sell a bobble head of Tarkington with every copy.

"I got another idea. I'm working on it. I'm gonna get a database of rare book collectors, and I'm just gonna ask them if I could have a book. It wouldn't hurt to ask. I mean, I'm trying not to do anything illegal."

"You can't stop, can you?" I asked, but it wasn't really a question.

"I just like to collect books, collect stuff. Actually, I was gonna tell you about a new plan that I have, but I guess I better not. I'll tell you later. I don't want to do anything criminal, 'cause I don't want to go back to prison. But somehow, if I can get my books for free, it would be better."

The next time we met, when I was almost accustomed to Gilkey's eagerness to contribute to his own story, he surprised me. Speculating that maybe there wasn't enough action in the book I was writing, he looked at me with a quizzical expression and asked, "So, do you think I should get all one hundred books now?"

"I'm not going to answer that question," I said, stunned.

He had begun orchestrating his life with an eye to how it might appear on the printed page, but I was still trying to cling to the notion that I was recording a story that was progressing without my influence. I was not going to become its director.

Gilkey elaborated on his reasoning.

"I was trying to think of a grand finale . . ." he said. "Getting a hundred books from that one-hundred-books list. To say that I had won."

I was astounded, but I was also at ease, a dawning that came to me unexpectedly. Nearing the end of my encounters with Gilkey, what was once tense and awkward had become routine, sometimes even pleasurable. He loved books; this we had in common. Over the course of a couple of years, I had sat across numerous café tables from him and listened to him tell his story. What became clear was that although he was a criminal, he was also curious, ambitious, and polite, three qualities I respect. But later, at home, I would listen to our taped conversations and realize how the con man's physical presence had distracted me from the content of his narratives. The surface charm of a con man, like most enchantments, is a form of manipulation, and behind the façade stood a sturdy buttress of greed.

Once, after Gilkey had told me about a book he stole and later sold, he said, "Greed is greed." I had assumed that he was referring to his own motivation, until his next comment.

"Dealers can't resist buying them." He had mentioned a dealer in San Francisco, but wouldn't give me the man's name. According to Gilkey, the dealer regularly bought books and other collectibles from him at a fraction of their market value on those rare instances when Gilkey needed cash. The dealer told him more than once that he ought to stop. He knew the goods were hot, yet he bought them, no doubt confirming Gilkey's conviction that many in the trade are corrupt. I asked for the dealer's name again, but Gilkey declined. Greed is greed.[3]

❖ ❖

ONE OF THE most astonishing books I ever encountered was at a book fair. I can't remember the title or any other detail, except one. The dealer picked up the gilt-edged book and, holding it in front of me, slowly bent the block of pages as though he was about to fan through it in search of something. As he bent the pages, the gilt edge disappeared, revealing, along the long side, an intricate painting of a nautical scene, men navigating a stormy sea. "It's a fore-edge painting," he said. I gawked, then asked him to do it again. I learned that for centuries, artisans have been adorning books with fore-edge paintings for clients. They are delicately executed images, usually thematically related to the text: elaborate battle scenes, presidential portraits, Art Deco beauties, even erotic renderings, which, given the paintings' clandestine quality, is no surprise. As if one hidden treasure were not enough, books are sometimes painted with two fore-edge images, so that when you bend the block of pages one way, one picture emerges, but when you bend it the other way, another appears. They are not usually applied to highly valuable books (doing so would be regarded as a form of vandalism) but to books that are of special interest or sentimental value to their owners. Emerging unexpectedly, these paintings seem like magical apparitions, as though bending a book's pages can make the inert black type within metamorphose into sumptuous color images. When the pages, no longer swayed, are back in place, no one would guess what lies just a hair's distance beyond the gilt.

After two years of meeting with Gilkey I'd seen the gilt pages of his book, so to speak, and I had been witness to their being fanned one way, then another. If I had to reduce him to a sentence, I'd say that Gilkey is a man who believes that the ownership of a vast rare book collection would be the ultimate expression of his identity, that any means of getting it would be fair and right, and that once people could see his collection, they would appreciate the man who had built it.

But he was more than that. I listened to the tapes of our conversations repeatedly, and each time, Gilkey's selfishness, which in person is thickly veiled by his affable de-

savored being around so much beauty and, even more, appreciated the stories behind the books. In my reading, one aspect of the history of books I had come across repeatedly was their destruction. From the Qin Shi Huang in China, who in 213 B.C. ordered the burning of all books not pertaining to agriculture, medicine, or prophecy,[4] to the Nazis' literary cleansing by fire (*Säuberung*) of twenty-five thousand volumes, totalitarian leaders have acted against books' dangerous power to enlighten. Even today, some U.S. leaders attempt the same through banning books. So the fact that any ancient text, like the German *Kräutterbuch* my friend lent me, has survived is all the more heartening. The fearsome urge to destroy or suppress books is an acknowledgment of their power, and not only that of august scientific, political, and philosophical texts but that of small, quiet books of poetry and fiction as well, which nonetheless hold great capacity to change us. As I spent time among rare books and their collectors, as strongly as I felt this power and their manifold other attractions, I did not succumb to full-blown bibliomania, as I thought I might. I did, however, come to understand more fully the satisfaction of the pursuit. Hunting down treasures for a collection brings its own rewards, but, ultimately even more satisfying, building it is a way of creating a narrative. When books are joined with others that have traits in common they form a larger story that can reveal something wholly new about the history of democracy, or Renaissance

about a statute of limitations and stared at my notebook as if it held his future. For a moment, he looked frozen. Then he tossed out something about how the book might possibly hurt his future employment opportunities.

"But no, I'm not worried about it," he said, regaining his composure. "I mean, I gotta check certain legalities. Make sure I don't get charged for things."

Then, as quickly as you can slam a book shut, Gilkey, in characteristic fashion, turned his attention from dangerous risk to glorious possibility.

"I was thinking of the ending of your book," he told me. "I could write a series of detective novels. The first one would be about a serial killer who's fascinated by the poem 'The Devil's Walk,' written in 1820 by Samuel Taylor Coleridge. It is a very striking poem. It mentions bookstores and sort of an obsession. . . . Anyway, in my novel the FBI has to call in *the* foremost expert in the world of books and poems and classical literature, because there are no book dealers that can solve the murderer's crimes. This expert is someone who, as Ken Sanders says, went over to the dark side and found all these ways to steal, to accumulate the greatest collection of rare books in the world. And then he had to go to prison, but now he's out, so they called him in as a consultant. Unfortunately, he's a former convict. You know, slightly crazy, but he stole rare books. I would base it a little on me. . . . I'd be set up like this dark figure. And maybe I'd try to have more access to certain books that the government keeps hidden. You know, *the* book. You know what I mean. . . . There's always that one book you can never get your hands on. Maybe he's working with the FBI just to have access to that one book. . . . Maybe it's at the Library of Congress, maybe a special hidden book, the Dead Sea Scrolls, the diary of JFK's killing. Something like that. And maybe there's a surprise ending. Now he has access to the book, so maybe . . ." Gilkey paused a moment before delivering his ending. "Maybe still, I'm a thief.

"What do you think about that idea? Your honest opinion."

# ❧ *Afterword* ❧

I wrote most of this book from my home office, which overlooks a small garden of herbs my son planted several years ago, when he was nine. The only plants of his still growing are rue, a bitter herb that brings to mind the phrase "rue the day," and purple sage, which he once dried, then gathered into pagan bundles, and with a friend burned one night to clear the air of bad spirits. Both herbs occupy pages in the *Kräutterbuch*, the centuries-old German botanical text that led me to this story. My son got the idea to plant medicinal herbs from a book on herbology he requested one Christmas because it was one of the subjects on Harry Potter's reading list at Hogwarts. Like my son, almost everyone I met in the course of writing this book had been deeply inspired by stories, by books.

For three years, the *Kräutterbuch*, an inspiring book to be sure—but not mine to keep—sat on my desk. I often wondered, did not returning it make me a thief? Or was I a thief only as long as I kept it? Where is the line drawn? And having taken down Gilkey's story, had I become a thief of another sort? I have come to the conclusion that I was a thief of neither the book nor Gilkey's story: I was a borrower of a book with an indeterminate provenance, and Gilkey gave his story to me willingly. Many times did I "rue the day" I happened upon this story, and maybe I should have waved sage smoke around my office to clear the air of the bad mojo that comes with writing about crime. Yet I was always grateful that I had had the good fortune to come across such an enthralling story, one that raised questions about obsession and deception, how passions provoke us, and the ways we justify our pursuit of them. Like the rare first edition, a collector's longtime desire, this story had me under its spell from beginning to end.

❖ ❖

NOT LONG BEFORE this book went to press, Sanders, nominally retired "bibliodick," had nevertheless alerted colleagues of Gilkey's most recent theft: stealing a book from a Canadian dealer. Gilkey was not arrested. The story never ends.

This book belongs to none but me

For there's my name inside to see.

To steal this book, if you should try,

It's by the throat that you'll hang high.

And ravens then will gather 'bout

To find your eyes and pull them out.

And when you're screaming

    "Oh, Oh, Oh!"

Remember, you deserved this woe.

  *—Warning written by medieval German scribe*

# Acknowledgments

Without the support of Ken Sanders and John Gilkey, this book would not have been possible. Both these men answered my endless questions, a feat of exceptional patience and generosity, for which I owe them profound thanks.

Among the many others quoted in these pages, I particularly appreciate the help and expertise of rare book dealer John Crichton and Detective Kenneth Munson. My thanks go as well to all the collectors I interviewed, especially Celia Sack, Joseph Serrano, and David Hosein. And to Malcolm Davis, who shared with me the ancient tome that drew me into the world of rare books and then to this story.

Having the opportunity to work with Sarah McGrath was a stroke of luck. For the intelligence and insight she brought to the editing of this book, I am deeply grateful. My appreciation extends as well to Marilyn Ducksworth, Michael Barson, Sarah Stein, and the rest of the people at Riverhead. I would also like to acknowledge Nan Weiner, outstanding editor of *San Francisco Magazine*, who published my original article about John Gilkey and Ken Sanders.

My sincere appreciation goes to literary agent Jim Levine. For his vision, savvy, and faith in this book, I owe him a huge debt of gratitude. I also appreciate the hard work and dedication of Danielle Svetcov and Lindsay Edgecormbe, both also of Levine Greenberg.

Writing is usually a lonely endeavor, but for almost a decade I have enjoyed the tremendous good fortune of being part of the writing group North 24th. Heartfelt thanks to fellow members: Leslie Crawford, Frances Dinkelspiel, Katherine Ellison, Sharon Epel, Susan Freinkel, Katherine Neilan, Lisa Wallgren Okuhn, and Jill Storey.

I thank everyone at the San Francisco Writers' Grotto, particularly Natalie Baszile and Melanie Gideon. I am indebted as well to Andy Keiffer, Ursula Bendixon, and Waltraud Bendixon, and to my parents, Lyle and Sidney Hoover, for their help and encouragement.

While writing this book, I have been grateful for my children, Sonja and Julian, whose incessant hunger for stories of book theft often kept me going. And to John, for his support and unflagging belief, I owe special thanks and love.

# Notes

A fellow writer once described to me the experience of falling into "research rapture." While working on this book I succumbed, wholeheartedly. While I relied heavily on the written word (books, periodicals, Internet resources, and so forth) for historical information about the antiquarian book trade, face-to-face interviews (with dealers, librarians, collectors, and others) constituted the majority of my research. Scenes from the lives of Ken Sanders and John Gilkey, especially, were drawn almost exclusively from my conversations with them, with additional information culled from interviews with their relatives, friends, and colleagues. Court documents and police records were also invaluable. And every month or so, I would come across another report of book theft in the press, which underscored for me how prevalent the crime is and how, for all its history, it is still a modern story.

# Prologue

1. Leslie Overstreet, Curator of Natural History Rare Books, Smithsonian Institution Libraries, e-mail correspondence with the author.

2. Bock was controversial because he was a physician/metaphysician who believed that botanical parts corresponded to human body parts and processes. Barbara Pitschel, Head Librarian, San Francisco Botanical Garden at Strybing Arboretum, e-mail correspondence with the author.

3. John Windle. Interview with the author.

4. Ibid.

5. Ibid. "There's a famous story about a scholar in the early nineteenth century going into a fish shop in Germany. He saw them tearing pages out of a Bible to wrap the fish in—and it was a Gutenberg Bible."

6. Ursula Bendixon and Waltraud Bendixon. Interview with the author.

7. Copenhagen: "Twists, Turns in Royal Library Book Theft Case." www.denmark.dk (official website of Denmark). May 28, 2004.

   Kentucky: "Transy Thieves Took Names from Film." www.kentucky.com. October 11, 2005. This theft was unusually violent. On December 17, 2004, a young man phoned Transylvania University's special collections librarian, BJ Gooch, to arrange a visit to the rare book room. Once there, the man asked to see some of the library's finest books. He'd heard about the first edition of Darwin's *Origin of Species*, but wanted to know what other treasures lay in the library, and even called a friend to join him. Gooch had already decided which books to pull from the locked metal flat files and the glass case that held some of the more wondrous texts. Shortly, the friend arrived, wearing hat, scarf, and sunglasses, which made it almost impossible to see his face. Gooch had a bad feeling about the pair, but didn't expect what followed. As she reached into one of the drawers, they shot her with a stun gun, then tied her up and ran off with several rare items, including the Darwin, two rare manuscripts, and sketches by Audubon. "I lay there on the floor, weak as a newborn baby, while they ran off," she said. A few days later, the young men took the loot, worth about $750,000, to Christie's auction house. Their flimsy, improbable story raised suspicions, and the two were caught, along with two other friends who'd planned the heist. All four were sentenced to time in prison. University of Kentucky rare book librarian BJ Gooch. Interview with the author.

    Cambridge: "Biblioklepts," *Harvard Magazine*, May 1997.
8. John Windle. Interview with the author.

## Chapter 1

1. John Carter, *ABC for Book Collectors*, 5th ed. (New York: Alfred A. Knopf, 1973), p. 118.
2. Nicholas Basbanes, *Among the Gently Mad* (New York: Henry Holt, 2002), p. 81.
3. Quoted ibid., p. 72.
4. M. S. Batts, "The 18th-Century Concept of the Rare Book," *The Book Collector*, 24 (Autumn 1975), p. 383.
5. Ibid.
6. Readers interested in delving more deeply into this subject might enroll in one of several rare book schools in the world. The oldest and most famous is at the University of Virginia, which offers courses for adults on topics concerning old and rare books, manuscripts, and special collections. (Others are in England, New Zealand, and California.)
7. Collecting has traditionally been a men's game, but changes are afoot, according to dealer Priscilla Juvelis of Kennebunkport, Maine. As she observed in an interview with the author: "There was always this group of profoundly wealthy people, some of whom happened to be women, who collected books because

that's what people with inherited money did. . . . What has changed dramatically in the twenty-seven years I've been in business is that when I started in 1980 there were no women who were heads of libraries' special collections, with very few exceptions. And there weren't women rare book librarians. . . . Now there are women heads of special collections. There are women faculty members who insist on teaching Harriet Beecher Stowe as something other than a curiosity. . . . There are a number of women collectors out there who want to collect women authors, writings on women's rights, and the women collectors I have sold these materials to have money of their own, disposable incomes. . . . The atmosphere changed dramatically."

8. Since Updike's death in early 2009, the interest in and thus the value of his books have risen, as is almost always the case when a famous author dies.

9. Ken Sanders. Interview with the author.

10. Basbanes, *A Gentle Madness*, p. xix.

11. Ibid., p. 59.

12. Ibid., p. 62.

13. Ibid., p. 25.

14. Frognall Dibdin, *The Bibliomania or Book Madness* (Richmond, VA: Tiger of the Stripe, 2004), p. 15. Dibdin further noted that back in his day, the early nineteenth century, collectors were mad for (in order) "I. Large Paper Copies; II. Uncut Copies; III. Illustrated Copies; IV. Unique Copies; V. Copies printed upon Vellum; VI. First Editions; VII. True Editions; VIII. A general desire for the Black Letter" (heavy, ornate black type, the earliest of which were from the Gutenberg presses). Dibdin himself "craved uncut copies. To any sensible person, a book with uncut bolts is an abomination because it cannot be read, and yet there are many book collectors who will pay a premium for a book which is thus *virgo intacta*."

15. Rita Reif, "Auctions," *New York Times*, April 1, 1988.

16. John Windle. Interview with the author.

17. The suspect, Daniel Spiegelman, claimed he had supplied weapons to the men responsible for the Oklahoma City bombing, which meant that if extradited to the United States he could have faced the death penalty. The Netherlands' extradition treaty clearly specifies that if the offense is punishable by death in the country requesting extradition, it may be refused. After no definitive connection to the Oklahoma City bombers was established, Spiegelman was extradited to the United States, where he faced trial and was sentenced to sixty months in prison, three years of supervised release, and three hundred hours of community service. See Travis McDade, *The Book Thief: The True Crimes of Daniel Spiegelman* (New York: Praeger, 2006), pp. 58–60.

18. Basbanes, *A Gentle Madness*, p. 29.

19. California Department of Corrections and Rehabilitation inmate locator (telephone service).

20. "Brutal Trade of Rare Books," *The Age*, February 19, 2003.

## Chapter 2

1. Basbanes, *A Gentle Madness*, pp. 411–414.

2. One of the most compelling recent explorations into collecting is *Collections of Nothing*, by William Davies King (Chicago: University of Chicago Press, 2008).

3. UC Santa Cruz confirmed that Gilkey graduated.

## Chapter 3

1. Modesto Convention and Visitors' Bureau. "Area Information History." http://www.visitmodesto.com/areainfo/history.asp.

2. "Stanislaus County Is 'Picture Perfect.'" http://www.visit modesto.com/films/default.asp.

3. U.S. Department of Justice, Federal Bureau of Investigation, Criminal Justice Information Services Division. "Crime in the

United States 2007." http://www.fbi.gov/ucr/cius2007/data /table_08_ca.html.

4. Celia Sack. Interview with the author.

5. Gilkey offered another childhood memory. He said he watched a lot of television, and one of his favorite shows was *Amazing Stories*. The episode he remembers best is "when the mother keeps telling her son he's crazy to collect so much stuff. So one day the boy loaded up his car with his belongings and left. Years later, his collections were worth millions of dollars." John Gilkey. Interview with the author.

6. Dr. Alfred Kinsey, the famous sex researcher, who was a collector, wrote: "Most of us like to collect things. . . . If your collection is larger, even a shade larger, than any other like it in the world, that greatly increases your happiness. It shows how complete a work you can accomplish, in what good order you can arrange the specimens, with what surpassing wisdom you can exhibit them, with what authority you can speak on your subject." As quoted from Kinsey's *An Introduction to Biology* (Philadelphia and London: J. B. Lippincott, 1926), in Geoff Nicholson, *Sex Collectors* (New York: Simon & Schuster, 2006), pp. 236–237.

7. As quoted in Janine Burke, *The Sphinx on the Table* (New York: Walker, 2006), p. 290. Burke cites Max Schur, *Freud, Living and Dying* (London: Hogarth Press and the Institute of Psychoanalysis, 1972), p. 247.

8. As quoted in Burke, *The Sphinx on the Table*, p. 7. Burke cites Jeffrey Moussaieff Masson, ed., *The Complete Letters of Sigmund Freud to Wilhelm Fliess, 1887–1904* (Cambridge and London: Harvard University Press, 1985), p. 398.

9. Walter Benjamin, "Unpacking My Library," in *Illuminations: Essays and Reflections*, trans. Harry Zohn (New York: Schocken, 1969), p. 67.

10. Rick Gekoski, *Nabokov's Butterfly* (New York: Carroll and Graf, 2004), p. 12.

11. In 1998, the members of the editorial board of the Modern Library released a list of what they considered the one hundred best novels in English published since 1900.

## Chapter 4

1. Ken Sanders. Interviews with the author.
2. Susan Benne. E-mail interview with the author.
3. Patricia Hampl, *Blue Arabesque: A Search for the Sublime* (New York: Harcourt, 2006), p. 52.
4. *Bibliomania: A Documentary Film of the 34th California International Antiquarian Book Fair*. Directed and edited by Paul Ryall, 2003. An Antiquarian Booksellers'Association of America Production of a Session Seven film.
5. Eugene Field, *The Love Affairs of a Bibliomaniac* (New York: Charles Scribner's Sons, 1896), pp. 97–98.

## Chapter 6

1. Ken Sanders. Interview with the author.
2. According to Sanders, a complete copy was recently sold for more than $1 million.
3. James Thorpe, *Henry Edwards Huntington: A Biography* (Berkeley and Los Angeles: University of California Press, 1994).
4. www.huntington.org (website of The Huntington Library, Art Collections and Botanical Gardens).
5. Barbara Pitschel, Head Librarian, San Francisco Botanical Garden at Strybing Arboretum. E-mail correspondence with the author.
6. For a thorough account of the world's violence toward books, see Fernando Baez, *A Universal History of the Destruction of Books*, trans. Alfred MacAdam (New York: Atlas, 2008).
7. Basbanes, *A Gentle Madness*, pp. 42–43.

## Chapter 7

1. This was before the availability of Wi-Fi.
2. John Milton, *Areopagitica.*
3. Walt Whitman, "So Long," *Leaves of Grass.*
4. Quoted in Basbanes, *A Gentle Madness*, p. 20.
5. Tony Garcia. Interview with the author.
6. Ken Lopez. Interview with the author.
7. Kenneth Munson. Interview with the author.
8. Ken Sanders. Sequence of events reported in interviews with the author.
9. Kenneth Munson. Interview with the author. Munson explained that suspects will often use the physical details of someone they're close to when describing a nonexistent accomplice. In Gilkey's case, Munson assumed it was Gilkey's own father he was describing.

## Chapter 8

1. This is a common misconception, stemming probably from the fact that his 1876 *The Hunting of the Snark* is one of the earliest books by a famous author for which the jacket still exists. Earlier jackets from the 1830s by relatively unknown authors are still around.
2. Ken Sanders. Interview with the author.
3. Arnold Herr. Interview with the author.
4. Kenneth Munson. Interview with the author.
5. Ibid.
6. Confirmed as standard procedure for prisoners residing in the Reception Center by San Quentin State Prison public information officer Lieutenant Samuel Robinson.

## Chapter 9

1. John Crichton. Interview with the author.

## Chapter 10

1. Andrew Clark. Interview with the author.

2. Alan Beatts. Interview with the author.

3. Bob Gavora. Interview with the author.

4. This lax attitude was not always so. In the time of King Henry IV (late fourteenth, early fifteenth centuries) a man named Johannes Leycestre and his wife, Cedilia, stole "a little book from an old church." His punishment: "Let him be hanged by the neck until his life departs." Apparently, the fate of Cedilia, like that of most women of her day, was not worth recording. See Edwin White Gaillard, "The Book Larceny Problem," *The Library Journal*, vol. 45 (March 15, 1920), pp. 247–254, 307–312.

5. Sebastiaan Hesselink, interviews with the author, and Travis McDade, *The Book Thief* (Westport, CT: Praeger, 2006).

6. Nicholas A. Basbanes, *A Splendor of Letters* (New York: Harper Perennial, 2004), p. 15.

7. Robert Vosper, *A Pair of Bibliomanes for Kansas: Ralph Ellis and Thomas Jefferson Fitzpatrick* (Bibliographical Society of America publication), vol. 55 (Third Quarter, 1961).

8. James Gilreath and Douglas L. Wilson, eds., *Thomas Jefferson's Library* (Washington, DC: United States Government Printing Office, 1989).

9. Wilmarth Sheldon Lewis wrote this for a speech that was never delivered. Quoted in Basbanes, *A Gentle Madness*, p. 23.

10. P. Alessandra Maccioni Ruju and Marco Mostert, *The Life and Times of Guglielmo Libri* (Hilvesum, Netherlands: Verloren, 1995).

## Chapter 11

1. Lawrence Sidney Thompson, *Notes on Bibliokleptomania*, Bulletin of The New York Public Library, September 1944; and Basbanes, *A Gentle Madness*.

## Chapter 13

1. American Library Association online newsletter, December 12, 2003.

## Chapter 14

1. Marcello Simonetta, ed., *Federico da Montefeltro and His Library* (Milan: Y. Press and Biblioteca Apostolica Vaticana, 2007).
2. Jonathan J. G. Alexander, "Perfection of Illustration and Ornament," in Simonetta, *Federico da Montefeltro and His Library*, p. 17.
3. According to Freud, the collector's makeup often includes "an enquiring mind; a penchant for secrecy" and "a propensity for rationalization." As quoted in Burke, *The Sphinx on the Table*, p. 196. Burke cites Patrick Mauries, *Cabinets of Curiosities* (London: Thames & Hudson, 2002), p. 182.
4. Baez, *A Universal History of the Destruction of Books*.

# A Note on Sources

It's probably no surprise that there are many books about rare books and those who collect them. To read them is to learn the rich history of the book, the varied forms it has taken, and why some periods, genres, authors, illustrators, and presses lend collectible charm to a selection of them. Surprisingly few books, on the other hand, detail the deeds of book thieves. The bulk of this information I found in periodicals and by interviewing those who have had first-hand experience with them. Readers interested in learning more are advised to visit rare book libraries and bookstores, where they will be able not only to see, touch, even read, fine old books, but also to hear for themselves stories that have never been put to paper, never bound into a book.

While there are several fine memoirs by and biographies of in-dividual collectors, the following books offer readers an expansive view of the rare book world and those who inhabit it:

Nicholas Basbanes, *Among the Gently Mad*; *A Gentle Madness*; *Patience and Fortitude*; and *A Splendor of Letters*

Philipp Blom, *To Have and To Hold*

Rick Gekoski, *Nabokov's Butterfly: And Other Stories of Great Authors and Books*

Holbrook Jackson, *The Anatomy of Bibliomania*

Robert H. Jackson and Carol Zeman Rothkopf, eds., *Book Talk: Essays on Books, Booksellers, Collecting, and Special Collections*

Werner Muensterberger, *Collecting: An Unruly Passion: Psychological Perspectives*

Harold Rabinowitz and Rob Kaplan, *A Passion for Books: Book Lover's Treasury of Stories, Essays, Humor, Love and Lists on Collecting, Reading, Borrowing, Lending, Caring for, and Appreciating Books*

William Targ, *Bouillabaisse for Bibliophiles*

And this is an invaluable dictionary of terms:

John Carter, *ABC for Book Collectors*